Managing Severe Depression

Jan Winster

chipmunkapublishing
the mental health publisher
empowering people with depression

Jan Winster

All rights reserved, no part of this publication may be reproduced by any means, electronic, mechanical photocopying, documentary, film or in any other format without prior written permission of the publisher.

Published by
Chipmunkapublishing
PO Box 6872
Brentwood
Essex CM13 1ZT
United Kingdom

http://www.chipmunkapublishing.com

Copyright © Jan Winster 2010

Edited by Aleksandra Lech

Chipmunkapublishing gratefully acknowledge the support of Arts Council England.

Managing Severe Depression

CONTENTS

Part One

What's it all about?

Chapter One
Serious Depression or Melancholia?

Chapter Two
How Does Severe Depression Feel?

Chapter Three
Why Does It Happen?

Chapter Four
What Can You Do About It? - First Aid

Chapter Five
Medication

Chapter Six
The Physiological Factors – Your Triune Brain

Chapter Seven
Brain Chemistry

Chapter Eight
The Triggers for Depression

Chapter Nine
Accessing Help

Chapter Ten
Positive Thinking, Negative Thinking or Reality?

Chapter Eleven
Friends, Family and Loneliness

Part Two

Managing and Avoiding Depression

Chapter One –
Your Brain the Illusionist

Chapter Two -
Self Help

CONCLUSIONS

CONTACTS

REFERENCES

PART ONE

Chapter 1

SERIOUS DEPRESSION OR MELANCHOLIA?

Severe depression has sometimes been called *melancholia* – a depression which seems to have taken root and gained a life of its own.

This kind of depression is a monsoon compared with a summer shower of 'everyday depression' or a fit of the miseries. You might not even look sad if you are inside a deep depression.

Ups and downs are part of normal life, but severe depression isn't. As with any severe illnesses, relationships are affected by the depression. It is very hard for other people who a are in contact with the depressed person. The other side of depression and a lack of feeling may be anger or over-reaction.

A frustration is that you may *want* to do something but be *unable* to do it because of the depression. The advice you receive is of little use if you cannot take it. Trying to explain this to advice givers can make you feel worse.

Surprisingly, as discussed later, the much promoted 'positive thinking' may be part of the problem.

The unwelcome truth is that you are the one who must, eventually, claw your way out of the pit, the miasma, of deep melancholia.

This idea can be upsetting, as you intensely wish for another person to understand and to help you. You may or may not get this. The only thing you can be sure of is yourself.

The most important task really is to get to know this *'self'*. You need to know your vulnerabilities and your needs. It is 'your' depression – whatever theories anyone else has

But there are some things you can do which may help a great deal, even in the worst times. It gives you a good chance of stopping the depression taking a grip in the future – you will recognise the signs and can take some action in the early stages, before exhaustion sets in.

The idea of this book is to offer a few ideas which have worked for the writer and other people she has worked and talked with. Some of the currently available advice about depression is addressed to the family and friends – and many people do not have that kind of support.

Other elements of advice can lead to things becoming worse – such as to 'talk about your problems' – which can be unwise if the other person is dismissive, uninterested or responds with more of their own problems: and you will not know until it is too late.

On the other hand the platitudes suggesting that you try and think positive can be galling to someone in a very profound depression. There are some very useful books around, referred to in the appendix.

Take up whatever is useful and try your best to ignore those who have no idea what real depression means. It is very difficult to diagnose, doctors and other helpers vary in their skill and personal experiences. There is no

Managing Severe Depression

denying that it is hard to get effective treatment when you most need it.

You may have a vulnerability, but you can develop knowledge of yourself and improve your resilience - the biggest keys to manage and short-circuit depression.

Chapter 2

HOW DOES SEVERE DEPRESSION FEEL?

Depression makes us painfully over-aware of our life situation. We're sometimes told that we are being negative. But it might also be that the soon to be depressed person sees their life realistically and becomes overwhelmed.

Too much perception is disabling - a depressed person is always anxious and uncertain. You might constantly change your mind, unable to make decisions - about what to wear or what to do, even in which direction to walk. You may become over-sensitised to the behaviours of others and feel an overpowering sense of isolation whilst at the same time not wanting to see anyone because you cannot deal with another person in your personal orbit.

In a depression, your identity may be threatened, or even lost. The central part of yourself, sometimes called the "ego", seems to shrink. It is still there - there is a "you" which is not the depression - but it can't support you at this time, it is hiding in a corner somewhere, not wanting to know, not able to make any more effort. That core self, the "ego", needs to be rested, nurtured and protected so it can take charge of the direction of your life again.

However, we do have to recognise the ambivalence of society – sympathetic and yet critical at the same time, which makes obtaining help more challenging. A sense of weakness of character is implied.

Managing Severe Depression

But severe depression has surprisingly afflicted some staunch individuals.

Mother Teresa, in one of her letters to her priest, talks of a terrible sense of loss, untold darkness, loneliness, and a blankness in her soul.

She was certainly not known to be a "negative thinker", or lacking in courage or character - but seems very depressed, concluding: *"If ever I become a saint – I will surely be one of 'darkness'. I will continually be absent from heaven – to light the lives of those in darkness on earth"* (*Come be My Light*, p. 230)

Often, the depressed person avoids other people. There is sometimes a fear of your own angry reactions, because you are easily irritated. You know that this will not engender sympathy, so you keep quiet about it.

A professional musician, who suffered severe depression in her thirties, remembers:

> *"I was sleeping too much and having very realistic dreams, so that my unconscious life was much more vivid than my waking life! In the day time, I couldn't walk down the street as I was crying perpetually. If anyone came too near me, in shops or on the pavement, I had a strong urge to push them away or shout at them. I was totally paranoid about cars driving normally along the road. The headlights upset me. If a car slowed down, I became agitated and felt my aggression rising. I couldn't make eye contact with anyone. They seemed hostile. I was very isolated and angry, feeling that a lot of people had let me down. It was as if I was completely outside normal life."*

In the worst phase, which can last for months, there are changes of emotion and mood, alterations in what are called "housekeeping" activities – sleep, appetite, energy – and disturbances of thinking and concentration.

This deep depression, which is so hard to describe, is also hard to remember later. It is a trance-like state.

Severe depression can feel frightening and even like terror. There is a sensation of "shell shock", as if you have just been in a great trauma but cannot remember what it is. There is also exhaustion, emotional and physical, with no obvious cause.

You may wake and feel absolutely petrified. Depression is often worse in the mornings, and associated with early awakenings. There is a great fear of not being in control of your own thoughts; *"...my mind was dissolving"* says William Styron about his own experience (p.13)

There are problems in negotiating what for the severely depressed person are the complexities of everyday life – even receiving and making phone calls, or dealing with everyday domestic problems.

Deciding how to dress in the morning may be a major problem, the mind frozen and possibly blocked with repetitive, cascading thoughts. You might ignore ordinary self–care, like going to the dentist, optician or hairdresser/barber. This might be because we don't notice how we look, but it is also likely to be that we do not want the contact and the necessary hassle - or cannot keep appointments.

Managing Severe Depression

There is an overwhelming sense of having been abandoned, of being alone in an alien world. Such depression may come out as anger, anxiety, paranoia and 'panic attacks'. There may be an unexpected fear of fairly ordinary situations.

When you talk to anyone you're no longer really interested in what they have to say, not because you are being rude, but because you just do not have the psychological room for them any more, they are 'unrewarding' to you. This may be a form of self-preservation.

Some extremely depressed people, having more or less decided that they are leaving the world, who are suicidal, may even appear quite calm. This is the "smiling depression" which is so often missed, even by those who know the depressed person very well. One quite small trigger may be all it takes to be the final straw and 'permission to die'.

Press reports of suicides with depression as a factor often include a comment that the family or friends had no idea it would happen, because the would-be suicide was cheery and 'normal'.

Other people may be seen as a threat. You are not actually totally paranoid – you understand that there is no real threat, that the others are not actually dangerous. But the fear is there. Strangers arouse anxiety, even anger. It is very hard to tell anyone about these feelings, especially anyone, including health staff, you instinctively feel will be unsympathetic. A very depressed person wrote:

> *If I am walking along the street I don't look at anyone. People's faces seem very unpleasant,*

> *unfriendly, frowning or looking hostile. I know there is no one here who is familiar to me – they are all strangers. I feel as if I am made of glass, but I don't want to touch them and I avoid any contact.*

These are probably "panic attacks", and none of the health personnel seems to have explained this. This patient was frustrated by the treatment on offer.

> *All the advice I get assumes I am much better and more capable than I am. Most contacts made me feel worse. I have to keep telling them over and over that I am not well and they don't seem to get it.*

One man gave away his beloved dog to a friend – an unusual action and a missed signal of distress before he killed himself. On the other hand, it is really very difficult to prevent a suicide when someone is really determined. The best way is to encourage yourself to believe there is a way out – and that this depression is not "real" but just one way of viewing life.

The main feature may not be sadness, but pre-occupation with repetitive thoughts, an inability to concentrate. You may pay less attention to the outside world; you are less responsive and less adaptive.

Knowing this miasma of depression or melancholia, and your own vulnerabilities, learning some new ways of living your daily life, realising that other people - good people, courageous and very successful people, people who seem to have lots of friends and a great family, have been down a similar path - all of this may help you to resist its efforts to take hold of you now and in the future.

Managing Severe Depression

The main key is to know and care about yourself and learn the best ways to meet your needs.

Chapter Three

WHY DOES IT HAPPEN?

Severe depression is thought to be almost always preceded by a loss of some kind – a grief. It may be a death or other kind of loss. This is the *trigger*.

Grief is not thought to be the actual *cause*. This comes from a chemical imbalance in the brain, which is discussed later.

Triggers can be the repeated onslaughts of distressing events, or a continuous chronic and stressful situation from which you are unable to escape.

Even low level chronic situations, daily stressors, can be as bad in their impact as a one-off trauma. It is when you have no means of escape and a feeling that whatever you do will make no difference that stress becomes overwhelming and prepares the way for depression.

We don't actually know our limits are until it is too late.

There may be a genetic disposition to depression – this is still being researched. Or we may have been brought up in such a way that we react to adversity by becoming depressed.

We may have learnt to serve other people's needs before our own and in trying to please others, lose ourselves in the process. We may have lost sight of who we are.

Managing Severe Depression

Maybe we have already allowed our 'inner selves' to die.

Certain people can become exhausted by giving, adjusting themselves to the needs of other people, imbued with guilt if they do not do this, unable to accept that some of the people they help will never be able or willing to respond.

And the emotionally needy will hone in on them.

Guy de Maupassant in his short story, *Boule de Suif*, describes a woman on a journey who allowed herself to be physically abused to save her fellow passengers. Afterwards they totally ignored her.

In this case, they did not want to acknowledge their debt, and recognise that they owed her their gratitude. So they simply pretended she did not exist. Especially as they considered her to be their social inferior, they resented being saved by her.

A lack of recognition can be very dispiriting, as also the perception of repeated failures or rejections.

Overly empathic individuals may find that they feel put upon by others – they are allowing this to happen and then resenting it. Recognising this and suddenly withdrawing their support services will leave them feeling isolated.

There is a lack of emotional energy to deal with all the possibilities of interaction in a world which suddenly seems very complex.

Common advice such as to "phone a friend" when you need to talk is not, for many depressed people, that straightforward, even assuming they have any friends.

One depressed woman reflected on this:

> *People say," phone for a chat anytime!" but "anytime" feels like one of those polite phrases which are just confusing.*
>
> *If I call a friend, she may be out and there is an answer-phone – so what do you say? I just sound really cheerful when I leave a message. I don't know how else to sound.*
>
> *Or the 'phone might be answered by someone else, her husband or son, and again you will have to talk to a virtual stranger. I can't decide what to say, what tone to use. Do I say a cheery, 'oh, hello!', or shall I be quiet. It is all decisions. It is no use saying be natural. I don't know what that is. Do you try to sound upbeat or as you really are?*
>
> *And they might not pass the message on. Sometimes, I ring 141 first so they won't know it's me. Then if someone else answers you can ring off.*
>
> *Or then again she may be busy and say, "I'm just doing something, can I call you later?"*
>
> *How much later – it may be minutes, hours or the next day? The friend may have problems herself, and you ask how she is because you are polite and then she does all the talking and drains you further. You can't use the phone unless it is someone you know very well indeed.*

Managing Severe Depression

Sometimes when you put the phone down you just start crying and can't stop. I don't even know how much of a friend she is really, underneath it all. Does she really care or am I just someone here for her needs?

This woman has lost confidence and she has invested one phone call with a lot of meaning for her self-esteem. She wants someone to be there for her, and deep down is angry when they are not.

Depression has been described as sadness that has become pathological.

You might not have got something you hoped for. Killing the hope need not mean replacing it with despair but looking somewhere else to meet your needs in a new beginning.

Chapter 4

WHAT CAN YOU DO ABOUT IT?

FIRST AID

There seems to be a small part of yourself, part of your consciousness, even when you are extremely depressed, which can observe what is happening to you. The other self has been called your "ego" - your inner self.

You have to be centred on your own ego. That is not the same as being self-centred. You are not aiming to only think of yourself. But the ego is the basis of who you are, and it is there to support you, to keep you in your own world. You don't want to be too selfish – but eventually you do need to put yourself at the centre of your own universe, or the world will feel a volatile, unpredictable place.

We need eventually to assume the directorship of our life, to pull ourselves back into our own orbit, inhabit our own planet, take responsibility for ourselves. Otherwise, depression and anger can remain at the controls.

"Everything stays the same regardless of the effort I put in" wrote George Sodini on his web page before killing three woman and himself in New York during 2009. That's how it felt to him, with disastrous consequences.

Our aim is to feel that we are in the driving seat. We can't direct other people but we can learn to respond to our own best advantage – to learn to manage our reactions.

Managing Severe Depression

Ideas for preventing and "depression proofing" are developed further in the second half of this book

Some people have found it useful to actually speak aloud to themselves, in private: "Look, you are in a depression. Hold on for as long as it takes - it *will* pass. You are going to be OK".

The aim is to survive the worst part of a serious crisis, and to build *habits* for the future when you have a chance to stop it taking hold again. The onset of the depression itself is said to be an effort by the brain to heal itself.

Despite the advice to get out and about, when you are seriously depressed you need to keep yourself safe. Advice which is suited to the mildly depressed can be risky for the severely depressed and make things worse.

Many depressed people will not want to admit to the feelings of aggression as this arouses far less sympathy than depression – which is said to be aggression turned inwards.

You might need to stay in, to stay very quiet, to care for yourself and let the biggest wounds heal. Avoiding people is an instinctive device which may protect you and others. It cannot go on too long or you will become very withdrawn and start to lose social skills, but you may need peace for a while.

Even having to phone for a GP appointment can be hard - with an often awkward system in place (e.g. the writer's surgery needs to be phoned by 8 am on the day of the appointment) especially if you live alone and have no one else to make the call. Walking into the surgery, and then having the embarrassment of explaining your predicament with no hope of immediate relief, may absorb much of your remaining energy.

Most people, even doctors, need to experience something themselves to comprehend it. Few have the extensive imagination needed to comprehend full blown depression. This is understandable. Even the depressed person often forgets what it was really like once they start to feel better.

With severe depression you are in 'melt-down', as William Styron expresses it - tick boxes and scores are a crude and possibly misleading method of measurement.

Medication can alleviate the chemical imbalance of severe depression. It has to be the right medication in the right dosage. That is the tricky bit. It took six months for the writer to get the correct medication whilst hanging on to daily life by a thread.

Sometimes the effort of telling anyone else how bad it really is for you can make you feel much worse. It can be a mini-trauma to have to keep talking about the condition to puzzled medical staff. The writer was only warned about this through a commercial web site. And how many depressed people can complain?

If necessary you may even feel that you have to make up a story about having some physical illness which keeps you at home until you can get proper help. It is not always beneficial to tell others about depression when if they are unlikely to comprehend. .

Once the very worst is over, you can engage in something immediately beneficial– like getting your nutrition right. This is, of course, much harder than it sounds. You know what you are supposed to eat. Basically, it is lots of different coloured fresh fruit and vegetables with a good dollop of protein. And to cut down or cut out caffeine, such as in coffee and chocolate, which is recognised as inducing stress. But actually curing deep depression is not that simple.

Grief saps your appetite. But you may be putting on weight and look tubby and OK. You may be eating carbohydrate and sugary comfort food. Human beings differ from the animals in that fundamental way - we don't instinctively look for and eat what is good for us when we are ill.

You will need to use the depression triggering experiences to build up your self-knowledge. You may be able to learn to relate differently, see much less of some people, terminate a relationship, modify an occupation, reduce contact, or manage vexatious people without getting too involved.

It can mean becoming very realistic about other people and what they offer. As we will see later, it is *realism* - not optimism - which can defend you.

If you have children you need to take them to a place of safety. Do not expect others to understand. Just do it. Anything is better than harming them in a way you cannot undo.

Once you do feel better, as you will with suitable pharmacology, time and space, you actually cannot quite remember the parallel universe. It is as if a curtain is drawn over the experience, and this is a bit strange.

But eventually, and in the writer's case it was over two years later, you can start to look at ways to keep yourself safe in the future. Start applying some of the ideas in Part Two.

The essence is to eat as well as possible, get yourself to get out of bed and exercising as much as you can manage once you are over the very worst. Keep as busy as you can.

Chapter 5

MEDICATION

Some authorities and parts of the media have criticised the use of medication for depression.

Again the reference by such folk is almost always to mild depression. Anti-depressants will have no effect if you are not depressed. The wrong dosage or prescription will also be ineffective. The writer was helped by a simple change – but one which took months to obtain - from Citalopram to Escitalopram.

Once the serotonin has dropped below a certain point, a common factor in depression, it apparently cannot restore itself and medication is needed.

The proof of medication is in its effectiveness. If you are depressed, it can help a lot - as long as you get the right drug in the correct dosage. You might have to go back to the doctor time and again. This is undoubtedly demanding when you have very low personal resources already.

You need to get well enough to even consider the behavioural changes which the "mild depression" advice focuses on.

Just as you cannot stand on broken legs, you cannot force a badly hurt mind. You need first aid. There is more of this in Chapter 7, **Brain Chemistry**.

It is also a problem and embarrassment for many on a very low income that a prescription takes up scarce resources. (Some more understanding GPs will supply two months on one prescription). This is an area needing more attention. Deep depression is a life – threatening condition and medication is usually essential and has to be continued – even after you start to feel better.

Chapter 6

THE PHYSIOLOGICAL FACTORS

YOUR TRIUNE BRAIN

We know that the brain has three parts, called the 'triune' brain.

This structure is important to the understanding of how we react to things, and also why we get depressed. Responses involve the thalamus, hippocampus and hypothalamus.

- > **Lizard/reptilian brain**:- the original 'reptilian' brain governs the protection of territory/instincts/aggression. There are no 'family values' in the lizard brain. The lizard, and that part of your own brain, reacts – in a shy, hostile, defensive manner. We seem to get like that behind the wheel of a car.

- > **Ancient Mammalian Brain**:- mammals have to sustain family connections, nurture the young, monitor the social environment, as well as running their own bodies, which is called "housekeeping"; eating, washing, sleeping. The ancient mammalian brain sets the programme for our need for relationships. That is why we get sad or angry when someone seems to have let us down – they have broken an expectation of relating behaviour.

- > **New Mammalian brain**:- this third part enables us to use abstract intelligence and to learn. It has the vital function of enabling us to use our imagination to find our way out of situations.

Often our relationships fill us with disappointment, even despair and rage – there is some affront to the relating needs of the mammalian brain.

If the inbuilt urges of the ancient mammalian brain to nurture and to be nurtured are frustrated, depression is a way of protesting. It is a way of saying, 'I really don't like this'.

But no matter how positive *we* are, we cannot change other people. We are not responsible for the actions of parents siblings and friends – though sometimes there is an illogical expectation from society and the media that we might be (hence the attacks from time to time on the families, even the children, of offenders or other unpopular people).

Blame is not inherited – though feelings of guilt may be imprinted.

The need to belong is a powerful feeling, and it has been said that to ignore someone is the next worst thing to actually killing them. The impact of this is serious.

Guy Garvey of the group *Elbow* observed that some threats and even physical attacks come from those who feel, "If I can't have respect I'll settle for fear". There is within most of us a deep seated need to be positively acknowledged.

We can feel extreme distress if we have no tribe. We often spend a long time trying to find one and to fit in, rather than face the reality and loneliness of moving along.

Managing Severe Depression

With both an "emotional" brain and "logical" brain we can, with great effort, learn to harness the non-emotional brain first. We can then ***respond*** to events using our rational brain rather than just ***react*** instinctively - putting ourselves at risk.

When our basic relating needs are not met we feel sad, disappointed or at worst depressed and even suicidal. Rejection by the "tribe" in hostile territory could mean death – as it does with some animal groups. We are programmed to belong.

Societies which produce depression, alienation and suicide will not be the most friendly and nurturing. Depression comes from a certain way of living.

Max Weber, the founder of Sociology, suffered depression and saw the link with the kind of society we build and the depression some people experience.

We cannot determine the family into which we are born, the quality of the early nurturing. Early experience affects the shape of our brains, creates and diminishes certain abilities in relating. We can use our learning and our higher intelligence to work with what we have and make it the best it can be.

Chapter 7

BRAIN CHEMISTRY

The brain is constantly trying to make sense of the world, to understand what is happening.

Systemic stress depletes the chemicals **norepinephrine** and **serotonin** and increases the level of cortisol. If you are very seriously depressed, you may not be able to get better without medication.

There are some derisory comments made that these are "happy pills". But becoming happy or even cheerful is not the aim. Medication with appropriate selective serotonin release inhibitors (SSRIs) prevents the naturally produced serotonin being 'lost' from the brain. It can help to avoid the grip of a down swing of mood. The effect of anti-depressant medication is to reduce the centres of vulnerability in the brain – a bit like closing the bulk heads on the Titanic to stop it getting flooded and sinking.

With serious depression, once you have hit that very low point, a bit more effort, relaxation or positive thinking will not be enough to 'cheer you up' and restore you to health. And you cannot take the "good advice" which is offered as you are frozen in your own world.

Your learning for the future is not to hit that lowest point if you can possibly avoid it, to watch out for it and use all the methods you can to stop it taking a grip.

Melatonin is produced in our brains during darkness, and switches off with the light. Too much melatonin can be dispiriting.

Managing Severe Depression

The *sun* is a key means of setting the biological clock. The sun seems to have a universal benefit and it is free. Even on a dull day there is some of it. Getting out in the light is one way of restoring a balance. With severe depression, it is not enough for a cure but it is an important means of supporting good health.

Genetics may play a part. A defective control mechanism in the face of intense emotional distress can turn on the adrenal alarm system – the hypothalamic pituitary. It is then very slow to turn off.

Once this unhappy *neuronal link* is established in our brains, we then automatically access the negative feelings when we are "reminded" of them, for example, when we experience another loss. We have become vulnerable.

In depression, the mood comes first. Having got into a depressed frame of mind, the memories are "recruited" to justify the mood.

These memories are not the trigger for depression, but the result of it. It is as if we start to cry - and then think of reasons to cry. In the same way, raising your voice can make you feel angry (one reason deaf/hard of hearing people sometimes get a raw deal).

Behaviour has a strong effect on emotion, as well as the reverse.

Some people have a long history of sad events and misfortunes. They have been unlucky in life's lottery.

Such bad events, the sources of grief, may not have directly "caused" the depression, but they do make you very vulnerable – especially if they arrive rapidly, with no time to recover or assimilate the shocks, and where you lack proper support.

Changes can occur. But first the problem must be understood not underestimated. Knowing yourself and what you need is essential.

Support the brain through the body with diet and exercise, as part of everyday life and guard it well – as if you had another life threatening illness such as diabetes or heart trouble.

You need to monitor your reactions – and, based on that self awareness, assess the life situations and associations which you need to accept, reduce, eliminate, avoid or increase.

Chapter 8

THE TRIGGERS FOR DEPRESSION

➢ Loss and Grief

"No one ever told me grief felt so like fear"
CS Lewis, *A Grief Observed,* 1961

We can pick out preceding events – something major happens, or there are a series of setbacks – leading up to depression. These events are triggers – they do not actually *cause* the depression.

Grief, "unresolved mourning", is now thought to be one of the main precipitants of depression.

Depression can be triggered by all kinds of grief and severe life stresses - any experience which threatens our capacity to cope. Depression means that signals are being given out – 'I need help'. But many of us live in a segment of society which cannot de-code these signals very easily, or help the 'signaller'. We live in a very private set of boxes.

Some events have a profound impact on our spirits. The main one is loss of an emotional attachment, leading to profound grief. Loss might be through events and situations - death, divorce, long term illness - or more subtle processes such as "growing out of" our friends. The death may not be of a human being, but a much-loved companion animal. The impact of this loss can be harder to admit to others, or for them to understand. Again most people cannot comprehend things not experienced.

When we lose a loved one, we have lost part of ourselves. But we also experience ambivalence or mixed feelings towards any loved person. They may have let us down, not appreciated us or met the needs we hoped they would. Affection and hostility are closely linked.

Loss, bereavement, divorce, physical illness or injury, disappointment, ageing or the onset of disability, may mean that one kind of life is ending. Our world must re-align itself.

The individual may not have had time to get over the loss - to "process" it. Then something else may happen. As the setbacks build up, the coping capacity can break down. Fear and trauma may take over.

These losses are themselves not a *cause* of depression. But they may start a spiral of self–neglect, insecurity, and morbid thoughts. The depression can be triggered by one 'last straw'.

Melancholia is the very dark side of depression. *"In mourning, we grieve the dead; in melancholia we die with them."* (Darian Leader p. 8) Depression is said to be the result of unresolved mourning.

The mammalian brain (Chapter 6) means that we are programmed emotionally be part of a family, group or tribe. When we lose our feeling of being connected to social groups we feel emptied and isolated.

The person who is depressed may not have been caring for themselves even before the depression. Or, far from being 'negative' thinkers, they may not have known when to quit. Some may have over-invested in the welfare or opinions of other people, gaining their identity through others.

The *trigger* is the situation or event before you become depressed which is linked to the depression. And the triggers prepare the ground for depression to take root.

➢ Broken Attachment

The reaction in severe depression is noted by John Bowlby in his work on *attachment theory* some years ago.

He observed abandoned babies where the child at first cries vigorously, expressing distress and anger, and then falls silent. The child appears to accept its fate – but has actually become withdrawn and depressed.

Bowlby called this *"frozen watchfulness"* - the heartbreaking sight of a child who has lost all hope of being loved. That child element is inside the adult too. We become emotionally frozen, that is, depressed, lacking in hope, in motivation, in a sense of future.

Your own repeated efforts seem to make no difference, and suddenly, without your own volition, the brake has been applied – a feeling of disconnection, loss of nerve and self-doubt takes over.

A lot of unhappiness comes from our interpretation of the way people behave towards us, or puzzling about the reasons for their behaviour.. Strangely enough, other people themselves often do not know, consciously, why they behave in the way they do. They are governed by their own unconscious motives. We can all almost always give a reason for behaviours if asked to do so – but it does not mean it is the right reason. But managing the disappointment engendered by the behaviour of "the other" can take us down to a lower level of coping

It does seem that perhaps with some psychological vulnerability from early life - perhaps deprivation or rejection - any subsequent trauma can easily resurrect these earlier problems and fire off the 'depression' neurons.

➢ Over Exertion

Trying very hard under impossible circumstances, perhaps being *too* positive, has consequences. In his novel, *Love and War in the Appenines*, Eric Newby writes:

> *"That night something happened to me on the mountain. The weight of the rice coupled with the awful cough which I had to try and repress broke something in me. It was not physical; it was simply that part of my spirit went out of me, and in the whole of my life since that night it has never been the same again."* (p 116)

This is the one last straw incident – it may even be, often is, something very trivial and "that's it". You've had it. You can't do it any more. Something – your spirit – breaks.

➢ Excess Empathy

Empathy is more involving of yourself, your inner being, than sympathy. You feel what it must be like to *be* that other person. You may identify with others, including their problems, almost becoming the 'other'. Early experiences and expectations might have built on this natural inclination.

If you are an "empath", and overly aware of the needs of other people, you might fail to draw boundaries between your own feelings and those which belong to others. And you may actually be unwittingly attractive to certain people who will not be rewarding to you as friends, who may not be able to reciprocate.

The empath may be attracted to challenge, or to quirkiness. Other people try to get what they need from you not because they are unpleasant people but because you seem able to give them what they can't get anywhere else.

A soon-to-be depressed person may be dependable, with a strong conscience and sense of responsibility. But their self-esteem may rest on the evaluation of other people. This empathic person will keep trying, and only after many dozens of perceived rejections may become depressed.

In the classic Star Trek film, *The Empath* (1968) Gem, the humanoid - played by Kathryn Hays - can heal other people's wounds, but only at enormous pain and cost to herself. She is used by the other characters because of her unique skills.

In real life the empathic person may get 'burnt out'. There are 'needy' people who will seek out someone, the empathic person, to meet their own needs, but such people cannot reciprocate.

There is a 'Little Pink Riding Hood' syndrome described by Eric Berne in his book, *Games People Play.* Because of her upbringing, Little Pink Riding Hood's sole purpose in life is to try and help people. She can only wait around trying to be useful, and then wither away when she is no longer needed. She has no fun and has nothing in her life which is just for herself.

In some ways, each individual can be compared with a planet, in its own orbit. As you relate to another person, you may be drawn into their orbit – which may be very different from your own.

The antidote may be to get into your own orbit, bit by bit, to build your own world – and to engage other people in that world with you, if and when you want to

It is said that those with good friends are less likely to get depressed – not much comfort if you are not in that category. However severe depression can strike anyone, no matter how many friends they have. None of us can be totally sure of our friends until the relationship is tested.

> ### "Anomie" – Being an Outsider

Over a century ago, the sociologist Emile Durkheim, in his efforts to explain suicide, formulated his theory of "*anomie*" to describe the person who feels at odds with society for any reason. *Anomie* is a feeling of not belonging, of being an outsider.

Times of rapid social change can leave people feeling lost. The normal community ties are broken. There are no longer shared values or cultural experiences. You are cast adrift and need to find some new bearings. We can live in an area for several years and not know the name of the person next door.

Managing Severe Depression

The privatisation of transport with the car-to-door syndrome, replacing walking as a main means of travel, the trolley-dash supermarket instead of the meanderings of the open-air market, affluence at a level where you do not actually need your neighbours to help with any material needs, a fierce protection of privacy, a decline in formal religious commitment, social mobility - all these changes have added to a sense of isolation – as well as freedom and privacy.

Another type of person identified as being at risk of depression is the "visionary" person, or the "artistic" character, who seems to need solitude even though it is often distressing. The presence of other people might be annoying, irksome or even painful. Not all outsiders are visionaries. But virtually all visionaries are outsiders.

Other kinds of people, such as the abused child or the survivor of a terrible event may also be forever an outsider; as might the achiever, or gifted person. One unspoken reason some people/children do not want to achieve is the often unrecognised fear of future 'non-belonging'.

Some have described the feeling of isolation which comes from the frustrations of what may be a gift, but also leads to loneliness, being set apart from those who lack that kind of 'artistic' imagination. This is part of getting to know yourself. An outer "skin" needs to be developed as self protection - or a persona - what might be called a *presenting self*. It is not a lie or a change of character but a way of engaging with the world.

The vulnerable depressed person feels a need to withdraw: the brain has become generally less interested in things outside the head and more preoccupied with internal emotional affairs. This can lead to persistent "rumination", dwelling on a life situation, including recurrent thoughts of suicide.

This isolation can also be the start of the cure. You may need to withdraw, to be away from the world for a while, to rest the wounds and start to heal. You are dying inside, but the seeds of the next stage of your life are germinating.

In the private car society, we do not meet other people on the street, and we may have forgotten the social skills of greeting strangers. An excessive fear of crime translates into a generalised fear of other people. We are no longer in communities where the old lady who passes us on the street knew our grandmother. There is no tribal link.

Ties based on blood relationships, ethnicity, a shared religion, geography a national identity, have become much weaker in some ways but also stronger. We move away from our families of origin – but we have less need of neighbours when we can drive or fly hundreds miles to see friends and relatives.

A certain amount of loneliness is the price of freedom, individuality, eccentricity, imagination, creativity. In that model village we have in our collective imaginations, where everyone knows everyone else, there is also more interference, constraint, judgement and condemnation - outsiders were persecuted.

There comes a time when we have to try to get outside the burrow we dig for ourselves in depression:

Managing Severe Depression

"... you cannot live shut in on yourself without paying for it. The mind grows rusty; interests diminish…" (Simone de Beauvoir, p. 69)

➢ Learned Helplessness

Learned helplessness (Martin Seligman) means that in trying over and over to do something, and failing, we can "learn" that the tasks are impossible and stop trying. That leads to depression or giving up – sometimes just before we would have succeeded!

In animal experiments, where distress is aroused but there is no escape, and no way to fight, the animal eventually becomes exhausted and makes no further effort. This is similar to a human showing signs of being depressed.

Because it feels as if it doesn't matter what you do, you may end up doing nothing.

Depression is thus due to the belief that taking any action is useless - nothing can be done. You have lost control over external events - due to bereavement, financial difficulties or chronic illness - so you become overwhelmingly sad.

There might also be a dawning awareness that our own actions, even our own competence, have not lead to a particularly contented life - one reason may be the taking on of impossible challenges.

'Successful' people take on challenges – but usually not impossible ones. Whilst
working hard, they use their judgement and match the demands to their abilities.

A good challenge has to be something which responds to your efforts and does not depend on miracles. What we are trying to do has to be realistic. You can work harder to succeed in a task – but you cannot work harder to change other people. One is difficult the other impossible.

You make the best you can from the materials of life which you have, modifying expectations but neither blaming yourself for the perceived failings of others, whether a disappointing friend, relative or child, nor dwelling on the matter for too long.

The "solution" to learned helplessness is to focus on something which *is* inside your control, resisting any attraction to a challenge which isn't achievable.

One reason for suicide urges is said to be an effort to get in control – as well as to end the distress. You may feel that you are not in the driving seat of your life. Maybe in trying to please other people, to be what other people expect, you become exhausted. The depression seems to 'allow' you to say no, it relieves you of duties. Careful, self-regarding assertion is better.

You may try too hard to please, but perhaps not picking up life - enhancing social skills.

Some religions are associated with a lower suicide rate: but these beliefs are often practised in
areas with strong shared values and often lower material standards, requiring people to depend on one another.

The antidote to this learned helplessness is to find things you can do. And to do them; to allow yourself the feeling of success.

Managing Severe Depression

➢ Disappointment

Dealing effectively with disappointment is part of grieving. One of the characteristics of those who become distressed is that there has been a loss, and preventing the loss was outside their control.

Disappointment is the reaction to an often unconscious expectation which turns out to be *unattainable* for some reason. Sometimes the expectations are actually very modest, maybe that someone returns your phone call. You cannot be disappointed if you did not have hope. The other person's different priorities, absent mindedness or alternative set of values may take on a profound meaning in terms of your own value. Maybe you don't, after all, mean as much to the other as you thought. Depression may mean you are identifying with the perceived rejection of yourself.

The person who has the greatest hope, the positive person, may be most likely to feel let down.

Anyone who some years ago watched the TV series "7-Up", following children from the age of seven to the present time, will recall a bright and hopeful little boy who as an adult ended up living for some time bereft and alone in an isolated caravan in Scotland. Something had killed his optimism. (He was later helped by another member of the series)..

You may find that you have accumulated people around you who are a bit selfish, lacking in imagination or simply incapable of helping when the time comes for returning favours.

If then the soon-to-be-depressed person does not recognise and accept this, there will be an overwhelming feeling of loneliness, loss, grief, anger and isolation when the penny drops. At the very time you need support, there is no one available.

The positive person, ironically, may be most at risk, the outgoing and cheerful sort who tries over and over and over again, instead of facing the reality – the disappointment - whilst they still have the energy to do so.

We often deny our instincts. We may pursue relationships which are not good for us, believing that with *our* effort we can make them work. In this case, empathy may well get in the way as we understand why the other person is not capable of doing more – and we don't realise the risks in continuing the relationship.

With the predictable failure of these efforts, maybe because the odds are overwhelming, come the foundations of a depression.

Some things really are outside our control. These are often the things we worry about the most. This includes other people's behaviour. We can only alter our reactions to others, not their behaviour. If we react in a way which does not meet their needs, they may stop seeing us – but that frees us for more nourishing relationships.

People very seldom act "out of character". We just get to know them better.

Managing Severe Depression

➢ Self-Neglect

This is a well known result of depression – but it can also be a factor in preparing the ground for it.

If you have exhausted yourself in the care of others, or in a job, or for any reason, you may have given your own needs hardly a thought, especially if the very idea of your own "needs" puzzles you. You may exhaust your self for other people – and then resent it, forget to look after yourself and then feel puzzled that no one else does either.

It would be good if you could pick up some of the suggestions in Part Two of this book as soon as you can.

If you do anything for yourself, do it as well as possible.

You may have to overcome a lot of your early training, and it will feel selfish and strange for a while.

➢ Anger

"Can calm despair and wild unrest
Be tenants of a single breast?"
(Alfred Lord Tennyson, *In Memoriam*)

Anger can be a result of the frustration and despair of depression. It can also trigger fear or guilt in the angry person and then lead to further depression.

You can be depressed and angry at the same time, as Tennyson says. Anger is the other side of depression. When depressed, you can almost ask the question, who are you angry with?

Depression as suppressed anger is also linked to unspoken expectations of other people, who "should" or "should not" behave in a certain way. It is linked to disappointment.

Ironically enough, it is the cheery optimist who is perhaps most likely to experience the deepest depression, and *"sometimes the mind turns to violent thoughts regarding others."* (Styron, p.47)

After the period of anger there may be a feeling of sadness and discouragement. But the anger is damaging and draining; there is a risk of injury to yourself and others.

Both anger and depression are linked to strong, enduring bonds characterising mother-offspring relations in higher primates. The disruption of such bonds is felt to be seriously threatening, setting up the chemical reactions which can lead to depression because a basic need is not being met.

Our parents/caretakers had a frightening amount of power over us. Love is nurturing, but there is damage when it is deliberately withheld, unavailable because of the parents' problems, or if it is corrupted in some way especially by the abuse of trust. . And it is now known that the brain develops differently if we are not well nurtured in the early years – including the part which makes us sociable. With guidance of some kind or from our own learning we can learn to mitigate this – but it is fatuous to underestimate the impact.

Blocked out fury, before the age when we had words, is the source of much anger and depression. Love and hate are directed towards the same people. These emotions can become overwhelming and lead to exhaustion.

Our technology has moved on - but our brains still work as they did in our cave-dweller ancestors.. This means we are not adapted as well as we might be. The emotional responses which have been built into us may be unsuitable for the present environment.

Anger can create health problems for us, physical and psychological; it can upset our appetite and digestion, muddy our thinking and, in due course, actually dispirit us. It might have become an automatic, unthinking reaction to normal, everyday stuff. Bringing it to consciousness will help us to cut it out – much to our benefit.

Fear, sorrow and anger are very closely linked. Anger and depression are sometimes seen as two sides of one coin. We benefit from a quieter acceptance of 'what is', of disappointment and frustration, learning when to fight it, when to ignore it – when to shrug and move along.

Becoming less critical – accepting daily nuisances - can be one key to dissolving a lot of depressive reactions.

➤ **Wishful Thinking - life inside your head.**

"Humankind cannot bear too much reality"
TS Eliot, *The Four Quartets*

To some extent, we are what we think.

When depression is taking a hold, the life inside your own head is more powerful than the "real" life outside. You may re-run real or imagined conversations, defend yourself, argue a point – your fantasy life is taking over and the contact with reality is less engaging for you than the world inside your own mind.

The real world fades away further as you ruminate.

We know that bereavement often precedes depression. One woman talked of her experience following the sudden death of her mother:

> *"I took on the responsibility for arranging the funeral, no one else would do it, and so had to come into contact with blood relatives who do not actually relate at all to me, or to one another. They either ignored me or just criticised everything I was doing. Over the years I had tried and failed constantly in efforts to keep some kind of contact.*
>
> *It just seemed to hit me that I had been doing all of the running to try to maintain these relationships. My efforts were doomed from the start, and yet I was the one who felt guilty, as if I had failed and being without a family was my fault. I seemed to go into a state of shock when I realised that I could try forever and it would make no difference at all. I felt betrayed by the world and all the things I had read when I realised that sometimes it's truly impossible*
>
> *Within a few weeks I had slipped down into a major depression.*

Wishful thinking may be seen as a form of positive thinking. We might think or expect that the world will run in accordance with our hopes, if only we work hard enough – without taking into account the evidence of our experience. Sometimes we have nothing to compare our experiences with – we might see abuse as normal. How do we know what happens inside other families?

In **wishful thinking** we don't want to know about things which contradict our needs and desires. With **realistic thinking** we want to know the truth – whether or not the knowledge is pleasant.

Wishful thinking – unrealistic hope and expectation - will link with depression because of the set-up for disappointment and loss.

'Positive thinking' can only govern our own personal actions, but we cannot make other people different by wishfulness – we have to use our judgement. Put another way, facing reality means letting go of wishful thinking in as neutral a way as we can. No apology, no explanation to others. Few will understand.

There are some ways in which wishful thinking can be a good thing. You may, for example, *imagine* you are an attractive person, full of confidence – and this can have a very beneficial effect ! A lot of success in life is through "acting a part".

But your capacity to improve a relationship which is intrinsically untenable is limited. At some point you have to make a decision about that. It is far better to be very realistic about other people than too hopeful. 'Expect what you get' is a decent motto. It deflects a lot of sorrow.

Facing reality is not "negative thinking". Depression may mean the death of one kind of life, to allow the gradual emergence of another, one which is more within your management.

The time will come to move on. Depression mesmerises us, freezes our capacity for a time, but contains a miniscule seed of a new and more contented life.

It is like a brake or a change of points sending us onto a different track.

Chapter 9

ACCESSING HELP

➢ **The General Practitioner**

General Practitioners vary depending on their interests, experience and attitudes to psychological illness. And help also depends on available resources. According to some accounts of depression, referral by the GP to a psychiatrist seems to happen very quickly.

During the writer's depression, despite seeing several doctors and mental health staff, this was not the experience. No-one even advised her on where she could get further support or gave her any emergency telephone numbers. Just making an appointment at the surgery was difficult.

She was told that the GP could not refer directly to a consultant (as with all other illnesses). The application must go through the mental health team. On the other hand, a pension provider, for example, demands a consultant's report, not one from a GP. But as the GP cannot obtain one, it is the classic "Catch- 22" .The only answer is private consultation.

The really surprising thing, to the writer, was not about these hoops through which she had to jump, but that no-one seemed to know what they were or how they worked. She had to research it herself and then convince the others who were supposed to be helping her. Advice was often contradictory. Responsibility for decisions was confused and never resolved.

Publicity for health services tends to describe the ideal – this might not relate to what is actually on offer in your area or with your GP. And politics can interfere unexpectedly.

Early in 2009 there were calls from army personnel veterans suffering combat stress to be treated "as a priority" within the NHS. Instead of allocating more resources for our Service Personnel there was a move to set patients' job roles against clinical priorities.

It was after four months of trying to manage her condition that the writer saw her first GP about the serious symptoms of depression. In itself this was embarrassing because of the publicity often given to the apparent triviality of the condition.

Staring at his computer screen during the whole interview, he eventually told her the mental health team were 'not much good'. Then he fished out a card from his wallet for a private counsellor. He told her to sit in the reception area to fill in a photocopied HADS form (a diagnostic list of questions to assess anxiety and depression) and "put it under my surgery door when you leave".

The GP did not ask her to make another appointment. She sat outside the surgery crying for two hours before she was safe enough to drive home. It took three more months to arrange a transfer to an alternative GP who was more helpful.

Some medical attitudes to depression are troubling. Another GP at a recent social event, referring to her patients who were depressed, said, "They just have to get on with it. I want to deal with people who are really ill, like diabetics". With these attitudes still around, it is a challenge to find quality assistance.

Managing Severe Depression

"It behoves a good physician not to leave him helpless."
(Burton, p17)

These were some of the issues uncovered by people trying to get help from their GP:

- The first challenge is to summon up the courage to ask for help. It is a very lonely journey. If you have no one to support you, it is very hard to present yourself as needing help.

- It is notoriously difficult for the GP to diagnose the level of the depression. Appointments with a GP are for a maximum of ten minutes. The GP assessment is, in reality, a hypothesis. S/he is not a specialist. There are many individual variations of ability, interest and opinion. Even if you saw a psychiatrist you cannot be sure of the correct assessment. The most depressed person may look absolutely fine – they are past all the emotion because they have died inside and may even seem deceptively bright.

- If you are offered treatment, it has to start on the basis of this very brief assessment, on a try it and see basis.

- The "HADS" assessment tool which is used to measure anxiety and depression - can be both puzzling and – by repeated use - irritating, with its ubiquitous tick boxes. Check lists should be only a small part of the assessment process, but they seem to be relied on quite heavily. This writer could not even comprehend some of the questions.

- Sometimes, patients who describe to the GP the aggressive feelings which are part of depression may be 'jollied along' with pacifying reassurances.

- Medication – even where the initial diagnosis is correct - will take some time to have an impact. The patient, already seriously troubled, can become worse in the meantime.

- The funding currently being made available for "talking therapies" is for modestly trained counsellors to deal with mild to moderate depression. Computer programmes are also being marketed, access to which can be prescribed by GPs. Like most of the self–help books, good in themselves, these programmes are for "mild to moderate depression". They are more akin to coaching the well than counselling the sick.

- Having to talk about your inability to cope can in itself can make you feel unwell. This is a hidden cost of seeking help which is very seldom mentioned. Both you and even the helper can feel it is a sign of personal weakness instead of possibly a sign that you could not say "no" early enough.

- Advice from some GPs and even counsellors can be, in effect, 'description and prescription'. So a statement or a statistic, or some revelation of science, or even clichés, are presented as if they *are* the treatment rather than just information or opinion: "we all feel like that now and then", "depression usually passes in a few weeks", etc.

- A GP may be allowed a ten minute consultation - but these may in reality be the same ten minutes each time, as you summarise how you are, and the session is almost a repeat of the previous one. Ten minutes cannot get to the bottom of a serious psychological illness.

Managing Severe Depression

There is also what might be called 'formulaic' interference. GPs are currently told, in the NICE guidelines, to prioritise anyone under 30 as this is an "at risk" group. This confuses the individual with a statistic and as such could change next month or next year.

The 35 year old may be the deeply depressed one and the 29 year old a bit under the weather. Professional judgements are needed.

Depression takes more skill, patience and time to deal with than more straightforward conditions. It is a complex matter and demands persistence and patience from the helper.

Even sensible advice is often unusable because of the very nature of being depressed. It is not that you do not understand. You just *cannot* do it. You are not "failing" to follow advice – it is just not possible for you to do so. When you cannot do it, you may be seen as unco-operative – which is like expecting you to walk on a broken leg.

Some advice is based on pet theories. These platitudes, clichés and generalisations are accompanied by an uneasy implication that, if these are not working, maybe it's your fault.

Asked, "on a scale of one to ten how are you today?" – does that test your depression or your stoicism?

Most GPs do their best. It is a chance you do have to take.

> **Mental Health Charities**

Unfortunately, even some Mental Health charities can give inaccurate advice. The leaflet from one of these optimistically reassures me *"if you would like to see a psychiatrist you can ask your GP to make an appointment for you".*

You cannot see a psychiatrist just like that. The GP is not your secretary. There are many constraints. In the experience of the writer, you are referred by the GP to a local Mental Health Team and the decision is taken by a nurse. That process can be very distressing.

There are a small number of charities campaigning for better services. But it is hard to get any "first aid" help – other than advice to see your GP.

It is striking throughout that treatments begin without a specialist diagnosis.

In the writer's case, the condition was labelled 'anxiety'. Relaxation counselling was offered, which was predictably ineffective. The consultant psychiatric diagnosis, privately funded by a previous employer, came 18 months later.

Depression itself can be a protective mechanism - you might actually need to be slowed down to prevent self-damaging actions.

> **Other Medical Interviews**

Much medical intervention in the form of assessment is not to help the patient but to assess for some other purpose such as benefits or pension.

Managing Severe Depression

The writer had to attend an assessment at a considerable distance of two and half hours across country. As she could not get to the appointment in time by public transport, she would have to drive. She strongly felt that she should not have been driving. She did not feel well enough - in an almost hypnotic state and unable to concentrate on any road situation.

The GP, having heard these concerns, unwisely reassured her that it would give her 'confidence' if she did drive to this appointment! A potentially dangerous driver was, therefore, released onto the roads. In fact, with considerable difficulty, for part of the journey the writer had to get someone else to drive her as she was too ill to do so. Some people have no-one to do this.

At the second interview, the doctor from the Occupational Health Department sat openly yawning at his desk throughout the whole hour's "interview", at times actually laying his head on the desk.

An interview for employment was carried out by a more courteous doctor, but he was actually an orthopaedic surgeon using computer generated questions to assess the state of the patient's mental health, and one which does not allow "contradictory" answers (if you can cook, you must also be able to answer the phone.) It is extremely difficult for a doctor to know how a patient will react in situations outside the serenity of the surgery.

Once you are really depressed you may look very calm. It is ironical that the sickest person may actually try to look their best to see their GP in order to bolster their faded self-esteem.

Some advice books give breezy, unverified assurances that the GP will offer a psychiatric assessment, or

Cognitive Behaviour Therapy. There is actually no consistency in this at all, and the help on offer will vary greatly from one area and one GP to another. And CBT is not a panacea for all levels of depression.

Trying to get help can be very difficult. But you still have to tell the GP what is happening.

> **Counselling**

People who work as counsellors have a variety of experiences, personal qualities, training, skills, aptitudes and interests. They have sometimes developed their own pet theories. Personality is as important as training in engaging with another human being. The moves to register counsellors will not in itself make any difference to quality.

The very depressed person cannot fight their corner and "demand" a better service. Their main fight is just to hold themselves together. Also, how do they know what the service ought to be like?

With a good knowledge of counselling skills, the writer found that this was worse than useless in trying to access help. Even very cautious comments, hesitant implications that the counselling was not helping, were met with a robust defence of whatever kind of counselling was on offer - an implication that ineffectual treatment was due to the patient's difficulties. The illness had to fit the available treatment. The patient then feels guilty about the condition not responding to ineffective treatment and despondency can actually increase.

One counsellor, employed by the NHS surgery, hardly stopped talking at all during the session. The writer could only sit in the freezing fog of the parallel universe to which she was then confined by her illness, and try to survive.

There is a human urge – which applies to counsellors as much as anyone else - to reach conclusions before fully understanding. And an insufficiently skilled counsellor can make things worse for the severely depressed patient, opening wounds which they are not competent to heal.

A far better approach with the very depressed person, apart from medication, may be to encourage some kind of structure and physical nourishment. Simply to listen, saying nothing is better than saying the wrong thing. But always end suggesting something of use to the patient.

If five people with mild depression find counselling helpful, and the sixth – the one with severe depression or having had a very serious trauma - does not, it will be seen that the counselling helps five people out of six. But they do not actually have the same condition.

A lot more very well-defined research is needed about the efficacy of counselling for severe depression may be needed.

In the writer's case she found it deeply frustrating, seeing a total of five counsellors, three privately and two through the NHS over a period of two and half years, that some were simplistic and made the anxiety worse.

On the last occasion and a cost of £75 – a week's income at the time – she was given yet another HADS form and decided the "counselling" was part of the problem rather than part of the solution. It was bitterly disappointing.

Some training of counsellors actually militates against this. *"Switch the conversation away from negative subjects and do not let them infect you with their negativity"* is the advice from one training brochure. This can effectively block the whole essence of explaining a problem! A bad event is not 'negative' thinking. It's a bad event. Counsellors may not know the difference.

The NHS counsellor may be employed to produce a 'result' in six weeks of one hour sessions. This process can be damaging. And there is no follow-up feedback directly from patients to anyone other than the counsellor themselves.

As David Hamburg notes, the response of other people is actually less favourable towards intense depression than mild depression – maybe because it is so intractable. Counsellors need to get the full story and not say so much, but we also sometimes desperately need direct, simple, achievable advice on how to survive.

The greatest benefit, which took almost two years, was finally seeing someone who was qualified and sufficiently skilled to be able to provide a professional assessment which was great relief and consolation.

> **The Mental Health Team**

Despite having been told by the GP that she would be referred to a "psychologist", it transpired that the GP could not make direct referrals. The whole pattern was of a confused, piecemeal and uncertain service.

There was a split interview with a mental health nurse, who remarked, "I've had bereavements too" and then said, "You look OK to me". Because of feeling so agitated, and even humiliated, it took the writer three hours to manage the one mile to her home after that distressing interview, designed to "help".

Some weeks later the writer summoned up the energy to write to the Mental Health Team Manager about this experience – the complaint was "acknowledged". There is no evidence that anything was actually done.

A few weeks after seeing the MHT member, the writer received a phone call from another counsellor. She was being offered six one hour sessions. The worst part of this whole process was the waiting, and the constant hoping that this time, maybe this time, there would be some help forthcoming.

If she was not well enough to attend, a session was lost. The counsellor taught her relaxation, which whilst OK in itself made no difference to the depression or her future management of the depression. The truth is, the NHS counsellor did not know anything about how it could be managed. It is too difficult an area.

There was confusion about who, GP or counsellor, should decide if she needed further help. The counsellor said it was the GP, the GP said it should be the counsellor.

The information literature which organisations put out does not always reflect reality. The writer followed up all the addresses in a badly photocopied Mental Health Team leaflet and none were of any further help.

They were all "dead ends". This is annoying and patronising. Even the address for the Mental Health Team office was wrong. Personal details could have gone to the wrong address. Compared with the glossy leaflets for some other issues, the impression was of a scrambled, cheap and patronising service. The local hospital trust is using leaflets which are ten years old.

The various questionnaires can be confusing. They are, or should be, only a small part of the diagnostic process. As one example, one question is about "losing weight" – but you may have gained weight and still be undernourished.

Few people are going to complain about the counselling they receive – they do not know what to expect and will be embarrassed to declare their problems if it involves mental illness. It is too easy to blame the patient instead of carefully listening to them.

The greater majority with minor depression or uncomplicated grief may find counselling helpful. Severely depressed people can feel worse afterwards. Some people improve, whatever treatment they have. This is the "Hawthorne" effect.

In that social psychology experiment, the lighting was improved in a factory and the output increased. The lighting was reduced and the same thing happened. It was simply the researchers' attention to the workers which helped - not the lighting.

The same is very probably true with much counselling.

In truth, the mildly depressed would get better even if the (now almost extinct) postman had a friendly chat with them. Many people do not need to talk about problems at all. They just need to talk and socialise in a congenial atmosphere – even though that may be hard to find.

Chapter 10

POSITIVE THINKING, NEGATIVE THINKING OR REALITY?

'Positive thinking' only works when you detach yourself from the outcome. Depression is often linked with *overwhelming disappointment* and a chronic *failure of expectation.* You might not even be aware that you have had the expectations until you realise how distressed you have become.

Comments about positive thinking can become put-downs to an already vulnerable, undiagnosed and untreated patient, almost blaming the patient for unsatisfactory thinking processes. It doesn't help and it trivialises the condition.

Contrary to some of the assumptions about a link between depression and negative thinking, the person who becomes very depressed may in fact be a distressed optimist.

Sometimes our lives have been such that many of our memories are "negative". The reality is that some people have sustained a lot of very sad events.

But, strangely enough, it is hope not cynicism which precedes disappointment.

The cynic, the negative person, the curmudgeon, may be less likely to become depressed as they are not 'setting themselves up' to be let down.

Dominic, a young man who has had two bouts of severe depression, has been upset by advice. His depression made him feel anxious almost to the point of panic and paranoia.

"It was very frustrating to be told to think positively when you have to punch yourself because you want to scream."

Our minds instinctively tend to focus on the unsolved, the problematic and the puzzling. These arouse the strongest emotions. When we have been disappointed or upset, most of our unfocused thinking can be "negative": interrupting such thinking by meditation or 'mindfulness' is fantastic if you can manage it.

The very depressed person, by withdrawing, might be making a serious attempt at surviving. This may be a reaction to overwhelming stress and a time to seriously take stock. This is an effort at realistic appraisal by the unconscious. The aim always is not to become a positive thinker, or a negative thinker, but a *realistic* one.

Thoughts may start innocuously enough. Thinking is not usually a conscious activity. It just happens. It may be a re-run of a conversation you have had or wish you'd had; a meandering consideration of events.

These are risk laden compilations, well disguised but often underpinned with anger. You have to find a focus, quickly, for your imagination, for your mind, your brain - in essence, for your life.

Thoughts are like the tentacles of an octopus; you may feel you are almost having to extract them from your mind one by one before they envelop you. You are almost tripping over them and unable to get on with the day. It takes a lot of effort and practice to channel these thoughts, to meditate, to focus on the "now".

Managing Severe Depression

The depressed person may pursue lost causes, unresponsive and complex relationships, debilitating marriages and friendships, long beyond any sensible period of time. They have neglected to build a hinterland of their own interests.

At some point there is a need to be enabled to acknowledge the loss, the devastation, the disappointment, to mourn, to learn new responses and trust in the self.

People who survive the vagaries of the world without getting depressed may achieve more by expecting less of others.

Chapter 11

FRIENDS, FAMILY AND LONELINESS

As Malcolm Gladwell reminds us, "success" in the life of any individual owes a great deal to the efforts made by a parent or carer. People who have been fortunate in that vital initial lottery of getting an A starred parent are often not even aware of having such advantages.

Others who are far less lucky often never recover from the damage caused. There are other factors, of course –being born with a severe disability or in a group being seriously discriminated against. But parents are the key for most people.

Both talent and hard work is needed, but intelligence is roughly evenly spread across the human population and the keys of opportunity, as Gladwell points out - are provided for the lucky few. Later you can make your own opportunities but children have to be nurtured.

Some children experience a more sombre "choice". Alcohol or drugs may be their lifestyle options, low achievement an expectation; echoes of violence cloud young lives.

And a child is "rewarded" – or avoids punishment – for certain behaviours. This may have been for being helpful, attentive and supportive to the parent – or even for being abused. We will tend to repeat those patterns as an adult. Being discouraged from meeting our own needs because of meeting the needs of other people will have a huge impact on our life. We may never even recognise our own needs.

Managing Severe Depression

In a similar way there are some genetic elements in vulnerabilities – we are still learning about the extent and impact of these.

We also know that the image of the happy, mutually supportive family is an *ideal* and not a *reality* for very many people, yet we so often deny the evidence. So, although most murders are committed against family members, we still feel, illogically, more scared of strangers. We continue to believe – to hope - that "family" means mutual support, and is essential to our life.

A teacher who suffered from depression, recalls efforts to get assistance:

"In the worst and darkest time, when I knew that had to leave my job, and I was also going through a divorce. I called my sister and asked if she could come and see me because I was feeling so depressed. She was actually annoyed with me for asking her. I told her I was at the limits of my ability to cope - and that I would have gone to the ends of the earth for her in a similar situation. 'Well, that's you, isn't it?' she said. 'You're just trying to make me feel guilty!'

It took a long time to get over it. I have to see her now as just an acquaintance. I was so badly let down the only time I asked for help It made the problems much worse."

In this case, the other person was not able to meet the needs – they roles had always been the other way round. Sometimes, you need to ask the uncomfortable question, *"if this person were not my blood relative, would they be a friend?"* It may be that Christmas cards are the closest contact you can bear. There is no point in fretting about that.

Due to your earlier need to get attention somehow - even at the cost of self-abnegation, of not being yourself, you may not be used to making demands. You try too hard and for too long.

There are challenges if you have moved away from your "tribe" – race, religion, your familiar settings or occupation – whatever key elements make us feel a sense of "belonging". This disruption might come about by choice – to some extent - as in migration, by following your talents and increasing your social mobility, or by necessity and survival needs such as moving out of an abusive relationship. Or people around you may change – becoming seriously ill or otherwise unable to relate to you as once they did. The result can be much the same: loneliness.

To *have* good friends you just need to *be* a good friend, we are often told. You get out what you put in. Not quite. Being a good friend may mean that you try to relate to people who, in getting their own needs met, are giving little back. They may be selfish or they may lack the capacity to respond.

Making friends is very much harder beyond the teens and twenties. Many people have their networks and families established and may not looking to expand them. Five year olds play with any other five year old. A few decades later, people become more discriminatory, consciously or unthinkingly, almost checking for 'tribal' connection rather than chatting to anyone.

Managing Severe Depression

A mental health charity web site notes that *"keeping your friends close"* and *"having someone to turn to for support is very important when coping with difficulties"*.

These are examples of *description* and *observation* posing as advice and insight. It can make us feel worse, and as if we are to blame for our alone-ness, that there are parties going on to which we will never be invited, rules to life's game of which we don't have a copy!

Friendship is not a reward for virtue, as is so often tacitly and overtly implied. The late twentieth century villains of the East End of London had hundreds of 'friends' whose turn-out at their funerals stopped the traffic.

You may know a huge number of people but have few who know *you*. Life is not always give and take. You may have allowed some friendships to drift. You cannot use 'advice' to turn to friends if you don't have those kind of friends. Some people may be using you in obvious or subtle ways, not out of malice but in order to get their needs met. You need to eventually stop this or to greatly reduce it without fear that you have to be either useful or alone. *You need to meet others by doing rather than just by being.*

The old joke about the man complaining to a psychiatrist that people were ignoring him and getting the response, "Next please!" is only (sort of) funny because of our recognition of the strong element of truth in that person's situation. To fully listen to someone is to pay them the highest possible compliment. As mentioned earlier, to ignore someone can destroy them. You might be surviving some heavy blows quite well – then suddenly a one time friend cuts you and that may be the final straw.

If when you try to talk to a friend they immediately started to relate their problems, this is not going to help you. The sympathy demanded takes what little energy you have.

You may actually feel much better when alone or sitting quietly with people who did not know you, just with people around but not even interacting. With quietness and peace, energy, the source of survival, slowly returns. Maybe you have become the kind of person who does not look as if you need any help. Listen to the voice of your own experience.

Without blaming anyone, reduce contact with those who drain you, limit the time you give to them and keep emotionally detached from them. It is quite odd that sitting next to someone in class when you were eleven makes you think they are your friend for life. You might well be theirs. But mutuality is a vital difference.

The pattern you have may be that the friend/relative/partner leans on you but never supports. ! People cannot change just because you need them to. The writer had to eventually concede that phone calls are seldom to recount good news or to truly ask how you are – often it is to off- load problems!

One woman was for some time an excellent and very caring, reliable foster mother. But she had what was then called a 'breakdown', having tried to foster an very difficult child. With no prior warning something snapped and she could no longer cope.

She told me, *"I knew a lot of people, probably hundreds. But I sat down thought, who can I call? There was no one. No-one at all."*

Managing Severe Depression

Because she had always been a coper, she did not have any of the supportive type of friends. She did not look as if she needed help - like the apparently 'smiling' lama or dolphin.

Even if they try, friends can also make things worse for you by saying the wrong thing.

Many people may think that they do have close friends. But, as in the bitter-sweet joke that you don't really know your spouse until you divorce them, it is only when you *need* your friends and relatives that you will learn their true character, reliability and value.

Trying to share a distressing situation makes it very much worse if the hearer responds casually - or not at all. Being ignored is worse than being alone.

Distinguish between friendship and 'good causes'.

Check whether you are a friend, a mentor, a social worker, a benefactor or some other role with each person in your network.

You may be unable to get support but you can retrain to prevent yourself giving it, if it is costing your own scarce energy resources. Go out, be less available, live with the guilt until it subsides. Do better stuff for yourself. Try to overcome the fear that you will "lose" the other person. You are just used to them. That is not the same as needing them.

You have to be fairly equal to be a friend. You cannot easily be friends with people who regularly fly off to Paris for lunch unless you have that kind of money. Or, on the other hand, with people you give lots of financial help to. Or where you are *always* the listener.

Meet others through shared activities if you possibly can – work, voluntary or paid, exercise groups or churches. The main thing for most people will be the interest itself – not all of the people in a group will be looking to make friends.

Your own aim is not to "make friends" – a huge barrier to leap – but *lots of acquaintances*, one or two of whom might, with luck, later become friends.

Also be realistic. For example, your neighbour may be "useless" as a friend but maybe she does have your spare house key for you. Just don't expect too much!

When you think of calling a friend, you need to know they will not make things worse.

One man who lost his wife did tell three people - friends and colleagues. He wryly commented: *"It was more trouble dealing with the well-meant but actually useless or even annoying advice. I had to thank them for it and then pretend to apply it. It was very tiring and I became much more circumspect later."* He was later known as a closed book on his personal life, but was very much more content concentrating on his chosen 'vocation' and the one or two people he chose to be special.

Despite living in a crowded world, many people feel that they have no-one they can talk to. This is not a new phenomenon. One from the ancient world is quoted by Robert Burton.

"...I live here (saith he) in a great city, where I have a multitude of acquaintances, but not a man of all that company with whom I dare familiarly breathe or freely

Managing Severe Depression

jest... I have not one friend to whom I can open my heart" (p.108)

Isolation can be a defence against disappointment, a retreat into a safer place. We can feel a "smouldering sadness", says a more recent writer, Peter Whybrow, where the world is seen as alien and hostile, causing us to withdraw.

You may actually feel apart from the real world when you do not have a happy background. Learn to accept it.

And in 1980, Mother Theresa wrote:

> *"...Do we know our neighbour....We have no time even to smile at them..."* (p. 296)

The ancient mammalian brain – which urges us to care for our families – also tends to exclude "strangers", others. For some people, there is no room for newcomers.

The writer, Rebecca West, also described the loneliness of having no support:

> *"Twice it happened to me... that people who were close friends of mine wrote enquiring how I was and what my plans were, and I had to write back to them telling that an extraordinary calamity had befallen me...on neither occasion did I receive any answer, and when I met my friend afterwards each told me that she had been so appalled by my news that she had not been able to find adequate words of sympathy, but... she was...my friend and would be until death... It however, only gives me a modified pleasure,*

it presents me with the knowledge that two people know me very well and enjoy my society but are not inspired by that to do anything to save me when I am almost dying of loneliness and misery......."

Even a slight indication that one person is concerned about our fate helps us to survive. So it is worth striving for that.

Start by making lots of acquaintances - and by making yourself *do* things. Most importantly, never "blame" anyone else.

PART TWO

MANAGING and PREVENTING DEPRESSION

There is said to be *"a window of time, a few weeks or months after a bad event, when we are open to new purpose in life, triggered by a trauma."* (Haidt, p 143)

Severe depression is similar to a virus. It may become quiescent but when it is virulent it is deeply distressing. It will overwhelm some people completely. Others may be able to develop some resistance. **Self-knowledge is crucial**.

You need to learn to look out for your personal warning signs and be ready to take preventive action as a matter of priority.

Chapter 1

YOUR BRAIN, THE 'ILLUSIONIST'

Even in deep depression your brain is on your side. It is trying to get itself right. It tries to make sense of the world, of your world. The exhaustion of deep depression might even protect you from harming yourself. We have assets:

- the resources of **memory** and **imagination.**
- a capacity to create new **habits.**
- an ability to **learn** what it is we need, what causes stress and what helps us
- personal control, with a bit of a struggle, to stop **responding** in the usual way.

Even 'reality' can be an illusion. A pencil standing in a glass of water 'looks' broken and a full moon at a low level on the horizon is an impossibly large illusion. Seeing is *not* always believing. The camera can lie, and often does. We perceive through the prism of our experiences and expectations, through our confusion, frustration and disquiet.

In another old Star Trek Film *"Spectre of the Gun"* (1968), the baddies – the Melkotians - transport the crew of the Starship Enterprise to the *OK Coral* of the 1800s where they are dragged into a historic shoot-out with a posse which includes Wyatt Earp. The memory cunningly used by the Melkotians to create the scene has come from Captain Kirk.

Being a Vulcan, Mr Spock is, of course, invulnerable. He has to convince the rest of the crew - by hypnosis - that it really is all in their minds.   Belief, faith, determination, thought control are all powerful forces. The 'bullets' are life's events.

Depression can create an 'illusion' of a different sort. It is that certain situations, events, behaviour, can be fatal to us. We are struggling desperately and we feel as if we are going under. We feel vulnerable, out of control and incapacitated. We are not in the driving seat of our lives. We can collude in our own destruction. If no one else seems to care about us, why should we care about ourselves?

To an extent, we are what we think – it is our thinking which controls us for whatever reason, maybe genetics, our early experiences or stress and trauma. Unless we *actively manage* our own thinking, it will take off on its own. We can lose the nerve to live our own lives.

Relationships which are broken by death, rejection and separation, or which are damaging and disappointing, become a threat to our survival. We feel angry about other people's behaviour which violates our own codes and threatens our values. People just won't do what we want them to! They are, we start to feel, rather stupid, thoughtless, inadequate, rude, unappreciative, demanding, dim- witted and/or incompetent. And we are? – we are doing our best, we cry....We can make ourselves feel like victims.

Learning a skill, engaging with the environment, changes the anatomy of the brain, apparently altering the synapses and connectors. And this may be more than a slight modification – as in the well known case of the London Taxi drivers, where learning "The Knowledge" of the streets of London gives the hippocampus of their brains unusually enhanced power

When we are deeply depressed, learning is difficult. But it is a cheering idea that such a vital organ as the brain is not fixed in capacity. We can even change the way we think. That is well nigh impossible in the deepest depression but it is do-able as you begin to surface.

Once the chemistry of the brain is disturbed, this affects our resilience and the way information is processed – as discussed in the **Brain Chemistry** chapter.

Depression may be *over-stimulation,* not, as the name suggests, under-stimulation. Our problem is that we take up everything at the same level of importance.

Recognise when the triggers are being fired – to delay or prevent depression taking a hold. We can learn to actively resist the condition *once you know your vulnerabilities.*

If your life has held a lot of overpowering sadness, it is hard to turn your mind away from those experiences. It's like driving round and round the same town, unable to get out, mesmerised by previous mistakes or bad events.

Much is in the mind. We can train our brain to heal and protect us.

Chapter 2

SELF - HELP

"Nil desperandum…it may be hard to cure, but not impossible…" (Burton, Second Partition, p.5)

When you get your strength back you can use your self-knowledge. Attend to your own experiences. You can do a lot to inoculate yourself against another bout of depression.

If it does happen again, you will know that you can survive it. Without any apology to or blame of anyone else, you can use your knowledge. You will know what is happening to you and catch the demon whilst it is still dormant.

You have to start from 'where you are'. You may have to reverse some of the cheering stuff which is offered as a cure for mild depression: When you feel extremely low, maybe you *do* have to stay at home rather than getting out into company.

A state of extreme anxiety and discord can make you a danger to yourself and to others – it may be that you cannot, for example, allow yourself to drive when in this mood. Get out later, when you are functioning at least at a basic level.

Advice to "share problems" needs to be carefully assessed.

Talking to anyone who is uncomprehending or uninterested, or waiting to offload their own problems, is at best a waste of time and can make things feel very much worse. For some people the words, "just calling to see how you are", are an opening gambit before they offload!

This does not mean that you cut yourself off. You just don't try to talk about yourself if you know from experience that it will not be understood, or even ignored. Much advice concerning talking to a good friend misses that vital factor: that you might not have one!

Nothing, good or bad, lasts forever.. You need a plan of some kind. This is a journey of getting to know yourself, of unpicking your programming and in a curious way the experience can change the course of your life for the better.

You need to feel a degree of control over your fate. 'Re-programming' yourself means that you have to decide what you will take on and what you will not take on – not just react "naturally".

Much of the stuff you are experiencing will be due to patterns laid down long ago, in early childhood. This re-programming takes time and you won't always manage it. But you will become more self-aware.

You may re-assess your relationships. But you don't want to get rid of them all. You can re-assign some relationships to a different level; follow up a dull but more reliable acquaintance. Some one-time friends may become mere acquaintances. It is sad, but it is the way to be, to recognise the disappointment and deal with it.

Whatever the circumstances, aim not to blame anyone else. Otherwise you experience yourself as a victim and dig yourself into a pit.

Managing Severe Depression

Here are some suggestions you can consider to make things better for yourself. Keep focussed on them to the very best of your ability, even when you are under the hypnosis of the depression.

We have to be realistic. The NHS provides a first aid service. The stuff we read about in the press and professional journals – that psychotherapy is needed alongside medication, is about an ideal situation, not reality.

Psychotherapy at the right level, for a sufficient period of time, with the right personality for you – that is a tall order.

1. Get the Right Medication

With severe depression you will need the correct medication at the right dosage. A chemical imbalance needs to be corrected. The writer resisted this for a while – because the GP did not have the time to explain the way the medication works.

Getting the correct medication involves trial and error. In the writer's case, this involved four months of ineffective medication, being repeatedly told "it takes a while to act", until this was changed by a GP registrar. There was then a significant improvement, so coping was better. It is very difficult to keep telling your GP, "but it isn't working".

A major issue is how you manage in the meantime – before the medication takes effect. Keep yourself quiet and safe. It would be useful if GPs gave some emergency contact information.

2. Sort out your Nutrition.

Everything you eat/drink gets into your blood stream, converts into nutrients and chemicals and directly affects your brain and your well-being.

You may be full but under-nourished. You may be snacking constantly – but never having a proper meal. Your brain is not getting the nutrients it needs.

The Victorian prescription for distress and mental pressures of 'rest, fresh air and good food' is still very relevant. You are looking for a permanent change, not a fad diet. Feeling full does not mean you are well nourished. It is quite hard to make yourself eat good stuff.

Different kinds of fruit and a range of vegetables every day is essential for good health. Mind and body are closely linked – taking care of your physical condition will support your emotional condition.

We now know more about our metabolism – for some people, that may mean four small meals a day. If ever you feel stressed, angry or very low, check on whether you have eaten – and what. Notice any connections.

Coffee and chocolate contain caffeine which can exacerbate stress – try (water-filtered) decaffeinated if you cannot give up coffee. But dark chocolate has some good ingredients too. And you're not looking to get slim but to stay well. Losing weight and getting fit are not the same – unless you are obese.

You may eat or drink things which make you feel unwell; you crave them because they are comfort foods.

Managing Severe Depression

Aim to put nutrients into your body which will support your brain in its struggle to get itself right again. Try keeping a food diary, writing down everything you eat. That action in itself helps you to eat better.

When depressed, for some reason you may go for the worst kind of food: you might have a small appetite or a craving to eat non-stop. You know what you need to have – the homemade soup and different coloured fruit and vegetables every day. Eating at the same time and place helps.

Food converts into chemicals – it does help your basic health and that supports your mental state.

3. Keep Moving

Exercise is the thing you least want to do once you feel depressed. Lying in bed or sitting around and "thinking" – ruminating – may be a favoured pastime. When you are in the very lowest phase, you cannot do more. But move around as soon as and as much as possible. You need to get rid of the adrenalin and increase the "feel good" hormones. It really helps.

Later, when you are a lot better, do more: walking, running, swimming, biking, anything which means action and focusing your attention. It may be best perhaps to avoid seriously competitive sports. Take journeys to different towns or areas once a month – once a week if you can afford and manage it. It all helps to stimulate the brain and so the resilience. Don't think you will enjoy it at first. Just do it as a routine Ignore hassles as far as you can.

One warning: some advice abut exercise is misleading. For example, taking a walk is a good idea, but not along a traffic-infested route, with road works, crowds, noise and potential for conflict. It is better away from a city centre where crowds may arouse your anxiety.

A walk needs to be in a peaceful place. The best is green and wooded, pleasant countryside, with a few things to look at on the way. Running a bit whilst you are out will produce hormones to improve your well being. Join a walking group later if you can manage it. just to perk up the exercise endorphins.....

A key source of melancholy is not being able to occupy yourself. The unhappy person often literally does not know what to do with herself. You may sit all day and do...nothing. It is not a happy feeling; there is no concentration, no energy, an inability to make decisions, a lack of purpose.

In time, you can do just one thing, maybe go out to the shop, just one thing to start off with. Don't demand too much, but demand a little bit. For those few minutes you may feel almost "normal". Keeping your mind occupied and distracted is vital.

Recently racquet games such as badminton have been advocated as the best kind of exercise. If you are on your own, there are dance classes where you don't need a partner. Yes, you do have to have courage to go to them. In a funny sort of way you are not doing it to enjoy yourself – not at first. You are doing it as if it were medicine, to get well.

4. Recognise the reality of other people: don't expect more than they can give

Maybe they "should" or "shouldn't" behave in a certain way – but they do! You will get very stressed if you try to put everything right, or if you get upset over it. There are different kinds of people out there. If they don't behave well, that is sad. The very hardest thing may be to realise you cannot change them. You don't strike gold simply by digging deeper in a gold-free zone.

Take the disappointment with several deep breaths and then look round for something else. Don't get drawn in and waste your precious reserves of emotional energy in worrying about things which will never change. This acceptance is *realistic* - not negative - thinking.

You may not yet have found your "tribe". Your talents may not have been recognised. There are a lot of opportunities. You need to keep looking. Don't get *mesmerised* by the relationships which didn't work. You may find that some people, even ones you are fond of, are "toxic" for you – you feel unsettled after being in their company. Learn to cut down on the time you spend with them. Have another appointment waiting so you "have" to go.

You may find that you have to terminate or ration your contact with those who drain you; monitor how you feel to learn who they are – that is the essence of what is called mindfulness. Observe your own reactions, especially your tensions, and then use the information to decide what to do, how long to spend with some people. Don't think that you "ought" to be able to do more than you can.

Learn how to rest and recoup, and also to accept other people as they are. Swallow the disappointment in certain relationships: remember it is not the other person's "fault". You can choose whether to continue the relationship as it is, or turn to other things.

You will need to find other ways to get your needs met, where your current activities are not producing results, especially the core necessity to belong, to make a contribution, to have at least one two close relationship, several others at different levels – and to be part of something. Learn to enjoy your own company too.

5. Talk to yourself

Constantly discourage your mind from focusing on things which are leading you into an unhappy state. Say out loud (in private!) "you are thinking about something which will make you unhappy. What you need to do now is... (e.g.) go out, or call someone, watch or read something - or whatever activity or distraction you can add in there, to shift the thought.

It is important that what you hear yourself saying does not make you a victim. It needs to be a 'good' reassuring phrase – like "OK, keep calm!', "slow down a bit!", "you're doing really well" (if you think you are) "you just don't *have* to get angry", any useful phrase.

You can make yourself feel better or worse by how you talk about yourself and the words you use about situations.

Try using less emotional words to keep your arousal level lower: depression is being over-aroused by bad stuff.

Instead of being "very annoyed" you can feel "slightly frustrated"; instead of "very low" you can think that you are "a little tired"; instead of saying, "how dare they treat me like that!" try "they are a bit odd"...And practice the shrug.

Take notice when your needs are not being met. Frame it as a problem, "how can I get more help for x...?" "How can I make it more likely that...?" Your brain likes a coherent problem and will work on it. A 'worry' is not coherent – it is not clear enough. It just goes round and round – as you know.

But always remember you cannot change other people.

6. Interrupt your thinking ('ruminations')

Matias Arranz, a Spanish Civil War veteran, reflecting on his time in a concentration camp, said that twenty people died every day. And the first to die were those who constantly remembered their families. He trained himself "not to think of anything".

Thoughts do have a "life of their own". The pattern begins innocuously enough, with a random memory – but it is not quite "you" who is running the slide show. The thoughts take off and 'you' follow them.

Eventually, if you are not careful, you have been led into a dark place. You need to deliberately occupy your mind as fast as you can with something else. It seems innocent enough, to 'let your mind wander'. But if you get seriously depressed, your mind is not safe to be allowed to do that.

Thoughts, the dispiriting stuff, the mindless repeated conversations, real, imagined or a mixture of both which go round and round in the head, the repeated patterns of resentments and confusion, anger and guilt, all need to be tamed.

One of the hardest things to do is to keep your mind still and away from feelings of anger. You may have to interrupt your thoughts every few minutes. This can be by speaking aloud, quietly to yourself – "get back into your own orbit"

You can try saying, "What exactly are you doing now (add your name) ?" to bring the bad automatic thoughts to the conscious mind to be zapped, and "Would you mind coming back here please?" when you notice your mind is off to a past time of frustration or sadness.

Maybe you sound as if you are talking to a dog – but that doesn't matter if it works!

But thought control takes a lot of practice, and once you are overwhelmed it will not happen easily. If you can, try doing it for only a few seconds at a time, this will help; blanking your mind briefly.

Almost all prolonged undirected thinking seems to become morose

7. Manage Your Breathing

When you have been upset or distressed, you might stop breathing for a few seconds. This can happen repeatedly and have a knock-on, negative effect on your emotions. Unproductive thoughts rage and chronic indecision takes your energies.

Although it is lasts a long time, depression is a lot like being in shock or trauma.

When feeling very low and stressed, breathing can be extremely shallow. To breathe deeply can even feel quite uncomfortable.

Managing Severe Depression

But this is one thing you can do even in the very bad times. Of course, you don't suddenly "recover" from the depression just by breathing deeply. The purpose is to stop you becoming worse, and to train yourself in something which will help you in everyday life in the future. It's just one thing you can do to feel you can do something.

These two may help:

- *Breathing in deeply and then pausing for four or five seconds, breathing out, pausing again and repeating several times*

- *Breathing out, expelling all the breath, as if from your abdomen; then tensing your muscles for as long as you can before breathing in again. You will then automatically breathe in very deeply. Do this three or four rimes every two hours.*

You are starting a good habit, and a first-aid method for stress and anxiety. It is worth finding and using other breathing exercises, and it is the basis of meditation.

Breathing exercises help to slow down the anxieties and give you a bit of peace. You may feel that you are already slow - but your mind is racing.

Try this every day and build a habit.

8. Use a "Chest Tap"

This idea is one I found useful – after hearing the hypnotist, Paul McKenna, talking about it - though it seems weird. When going into a really agitated/very depressed state you TAP the breast bone of your upper chest with the tips of your fingers a few times.

This small action can be helpful. Maybe it is because the depression is a form of hypnosis and we are breaking the spell. It is only a minor change – but it seems to reconnect with reality. It is worth a try.

9. Sleep

The best time for going to bed is two to three hours after your last meal of the day. . Seven or eight hours is a good period to allow yourself. Over-sleeping or dozing is not a good thing. Lying in bed creates the time to ponder and become melancholic.

This is the 'rumination' which can lead you quite rapidly into a deeper depression,

Listening to some kind of music, making sure it is the stuff which has a beneficial effect, or reading – if you can concentrate – or watching a film if that is easier, having a small indoor fountain of water to calm you down... it all helps – once the worst time has subsided.

Try very hard not to think or talk of problems before bedtime, even if you have to watch or read something scary to stop yourself.

Sleep may be disturbed by very active dreaming, discussed below, by early waking, or by an inability to wake up. This is a striking part of being depressed, and will get back into a rhythm again once you start to get better.

Some authorities believe that sleep deprivation can sometimes jolt someone out of depression. (Peter Whybrow, p.236). This may need to be carefully assessed. Preventing weird dreams is an area which might merit more research.

Waking up is important. One thing the writer noticed is the need to go straight into unsolvable problems and despair on waking. It takes an effort to say, aloud, "stop thinking and get up!" and even more effort to do it! But it can be helpful if you do not build another habit of disobeying!

Throwing yourself into the day – or at least out of bed - helps. Sometimes you are in a daze – but you are resisting the force of the potential depression. Those who have not been there will not understand the effort this takes. Try to find somewhere you need to go to.

This is prevention and recovery: you can't do all of this when you are really ill.

Focus then on **nutrition**.

10. Consider Your Dreams

One aspect of depression is that there may be powerful dreams which take a long time to wake up from, which may spill over into your waking life. You may have the same or a similar dream every day. The contents may be powerful and realistic. Then, when you are awake, you may feel you are living in a parallel universe.

The dreaming can lead on to the rumination already discussed– dwelling on things. It is almost as if the dream spills over into consciousness. Part of the pathology of depression is that while ruminating and pondering, the depressed person can become drawn further down into the melancholia.

It helps to try and remember that you can make things better for yourself. Dreams themselves can serve as a warning that you are becoming disturbed, that you need some sanctuary.

Sometimes, watching an undemanding feel-good type film, or - once you can concentrate - reading a novel before bed time can influence your dreams. It is worth trying

11. Accept your own personality.

A tougher suggestion! This means getting to know what you can and cannot do, to recognise and avoid the sort of triggers which make you feel worse. Some things can be confronted and dealt with, others have to be avoided. It is a decision you have to take. Do you try harder or do you give up? Is it worth making yourself ill?

Can you learn to ignore some things? You will know already what sort of things you find too challenging – either improve your skills or avoid these events as much as you can.

Try very hard not to frighten yourself with thoughts of how someone will react to your refusal to do something. That is not your problem. Developing this attitude takes a huge amount of practice.

Something from 'way back when' stops you standing up for yourself in an appropriate way, that is just saying with a smile that you don't want to do something or other, or you do want something else - without a fuss, just saying it, *without having to get angry.* But once you have done it a few times it will become more natural and be of great benefit to you.

12. Think about the way others may see you

Without being overly self-critical you can modify the way you relate to others, if you realise that this is causing you problems.

It might be that you offer help too quickly, or you might be overly critical (see below), maybe in an effort to put things right – two traits of people heading towards depression.

Also, and this is mentioned below, if you dress to impress you usually succeed, says Tony Lake... It seems trivial but worth considering.

"Successful" looking people don't tell you the bad things – they have learnt it doesn't make them feel any better. So it looks as if they have had it easy.

Maybe, or maybe not.

13. Establish your income base

Sort out your income if you possibly can. This is a vital part of your life. It is rarely mentioned in relation to depression – but there are very few illnesses or conditions which can't be improved better by having just a bit of spare cash. Only people who have never been very short of money deny that.

Modest socialising costs money. You cannot go out, even just on a train or bus ride, buy a coffee, or simply pay the bills, without money. You don't need a lot, just enough to get your basic needs met.

It is a major problem, obviously, if you have not been able to work because of depression. You might need advice on claiming benefits and knowing how much you will have coming in. The sooner you start, the sooner it gets sorted.

You can cut out some things by looking at what you are paying out. Small sum made a big difference. If at all possible, of course, increase your income to cover the costs. Check all your benefits – get practical advice.

Just setting up your budget and dealing with the numbers will help you to feel in control.

14. Re-programme yourself

You have to get yourself back into the driving seat of your life or even, perhaps, be there for the first time.

Use your self–knowledge and then try to live with the feeling of unease, even guilt, whilst you learn to do things differently, to protect yourself and be less vulnerable.

This will cause anxiety. Programming, even into an unhappy life, is comfortable. You enter a "no-man's land" when you start to change the pattern: but it will get better.

For example, you may have to learn to say no without any explanation or apology. There are all sorts of ways: "That sounds great, but no, it's really not for me!" or " I have a lot of things on – won't bore you with the details" Then quickly move on to another topic.

You also have to learn to depend on yourself, and – as noted – not expect too much of anyone else, to guard against disappointment.

15. Consider your pattern of criticism.

This is a complex idea: you may have had an upbringing based on being criticised. You learn this is the way to do things. There is though to be a link with depression here.

If it is combined with any urge to put the world to rights (as described in the 'Little Pink Riding Hood' syndrome later) you will feel a great urge to correct things which you see as wrong. It is almost a self-imposed duty.

The down-side is that you are also almost certainly implicitly criticising yourself, and may feel the disappointment in others which then leads you relentlessly into depression.

Everyone acts as they do for a reason and unless it is directly and immediately affecting you, you can ask why they do whatever it is they do – but that is all. Don't try and change or you will possibly alienate people and disappoint yourself. It is a habit which is hard to break.

16. Develop some regular 'habits'.

Habits can greatly help to see you through the bad times.

Because emotional life is so variable, it helps a great deal if you can form some strong habits: simple things like times and days when you do certain things, go to a certain place, times to get up and go to bed, whether you read a book for a time, and when you do household stuff. Maybe you can try to have one day a week when you do an activity – like a hobby - of some kind and nothing else. It is very hard to do this – depressed people are not good at having fun... You may have to learn that it's OK. And this will take time.

Some people are very easily distracted and impulsive. This is not freedom – it can make you feel very frustrated. The idea of having certain days to do certain things is not restricting but liberating. It helps to save time on decision-making and gives a ready focus for the day.

As soon as you can, sort out some structure to your days, weeks and months. Try to make some plans - not too much, but one or two commitments, times of day, days of the week when you do certain things. It all helps to keep you balanced and is, ironically, liberating as you don't waste as much time making, or not making, decisions.

17. Create 'distractions' – learn new skills

"Distracted from distraction by distraction"
T.S. Eliot.

The main thing is activity – doing something and getting your mind occupied.

At the same time as "accepting" who you are, think of the kind of skills you need to learn.

It sounds simplistic, but a lot of stress is caused by a lack of skills of one kind or another; not being certain how something is done, how something works. This does not lead directly to depression but it creates stress – and too much stress can tip the balance.

Managing Severe Depression

We know the brain changes shape slightly with each learning experience – and that is helpful. You need all those connections.

In *"To Build a Castle",* Vladimir Bukovsky writes of his imprisonment. Anyone who didn't discipline himself, who didn't concentrate his attention on some steady object of study, was in danger of losing his reason, or at the very least of losing control of himself.

In the total isolation and absence of daylight, monotony and constant cold and hunger of prison life, a prisoner tended to fall into a kind of half-conscious trance. The prisoner would then find it absolutely impossible to concentrate on anything.

This also happened to Second World War prisoners of war.

Those who found something to concentrate on survived best, even when they were starving. The Red Cross could deliver training manuals and examination papers helping the prisoners to keep their sanity and to survive.

Those who relied on outside events put their lives at risk. The writer was told by a former prisoner that a rejecting "Dear John" letter from home could lead to a man being found dead in his bunk the next morning. The mind is very powerful indeed.

Make appointments for yourself to do something,

 Keep trying to do these things once you are out of the worst stage. Until then you cannot do much except care for yourself. You may not, initially, be able to meet other people – take one small step, test the water.

Mikhail Csikszentmihelyi described his theory of *'flow'* to explain the nature of happiness. In summary, this means that you get absorbed in something – such as learning something or working on a project. You have to force yourself to start off with – like riding a bike. Starting is the hardest part.

And, again, this is for once you are over the very deepest part of the depression.

As you keep doing the activity over a period of time, for a couple of hours, you lose yourself in it, almost literally – the activity takes over and you forget "yourself".

So, what you need ideally is a clear challenge that fully engages your attention. You want something within your skills, but which stretches you just a bit. It's useful to get good feedback about how you are doing. Build your social network, meditate, and, if you can, practice a religious faith, if only to get more contacts. (Jonathan Haidt, p.95).

One of the problems with depression is a total lack of curiosity about the world as you withdraw into yourself. You have nothing at all to spare. The activity has to come later, when you are in a better phase, when you have more energy.

In the deepest phase you need, ideally, to rest.

"For me the real healers were seclusion and time…" (Styron p. 69)

18. Do some reading

Of course, that is what you are doing now. it is also a form of self-hypnosis. There are lots of self-help books around, and you will get at least one or two ideas from most of them.

You have to be feeling quite a bit better to be able to concentrate but books are useful and a comfort. The writer has found each of the works in the references to this one have had something to offer. Major messages are to occupy yourself, take exercise and eat well.

"You have to do something to change your repertoire of available thoughts" (Haidt p 35); *"half the day allotted for work and half for honest recreation or whatsoever employment they shall think fit for themselves..."* (Burton p.85) People who are bored need to get busy and the tired need to rest.

Studying and learning something can help a lot – once you can concentrate: a skill, a musical instrument, art or science –anything to focus your mind outside yourself..

Holidays with a frequent change of scene, fresh air – classics of advice but that is why they are classics because for many people they can help a lot. A number of people seem to become a little "nomadic" in response to loss.

19. Develop "apathaia"

Depression contains one message which is not that hard to interpret.

The way you live your life, the way you respond to events, the stuff you engage in or fail to engage in, the manner in which you look after yourself–these things are triggering distress. The crisis which led to the depression has shown this.

Depression spearheads learning and change if you will allow it to do so.

The demons of disappointment, anger, betrayal, loss, grief, all have to be confronted and, eventually, laid aside. If you have not been able to fulfil your own potential in some way, then depression can be a response this loss too – a loss of something of yourself.

Buddhist philosophy aims to promote detachment and self–regulation. The similar notion of **apathaia** was developed by the Stoics. The idea is that we do not let ourselves be affected by the behaviour, the opinion, of others.

It is vital to become aware of your empathic reactions – and to limit the exodus of energy, the burn out. It is an antidote to excess empathy. It feels unkind to think "that is their problem, not mine", but this is essential if you are a person who becomes overwhelmed by the needs of others.

You need to limit your availability by inventing some activity of your own

Sensitive and sensitised to the needs of others, feeling guilty if they do not help – the empathic person may need a short-hand way round this: a repeat of the mantra "that is their problem, not mine" is one method. This is very difficult, because we are programmed from childhood for certain roles.

If you have been in the habit of jumping in to solve other people's problems you may need to practice a less intrusive approach. Watch what people do, not what they say!.

You may have expectations of others which are not met – leading to disappointment. We cannot usually control the behaviour of others. We can choose not to see them, to see less of them, or to respond differently.

Apathaia means training your mind to become more self-contained and less disturbed by the actions and reactions of others.

When these things happen, you have to tell yourself that the upset will pass and that it is nothing to do with your value. It is a problem the other person has, a problem of social skills, or of unconscious motives – so even they do not understand their own behaviour. You do not internalise their behaviour but leave it with them.

20. Think about your personal appearance

When you are very depressed, you usually have no interest in how you look. And you may have been like that before you became depressed...

That is why the GP assessment tick boxes asking if there has been a "change" may not help. Possibly you have never really looked after yourself as you should, so you have not built up resistance to threats to your well being.

It is unfortunate but true that we tend to be treated according to how we look. If we look as if we are treating ourselves well, we are a bit more likely to be treated well in turn. There are some aristocratic characters whose self-possession, even if they wear very old clothes, means they are exceptions to this rule. They also have no concern whatsoever for the opinions of others.

For the rest of us, we don't have to spend a fortune, but it helps to spend some time to get the basics sorted as a habit – to clean your shoes (they are *always* noticed) brush your hair, use a full length mirror. Give yourself a message that you deserve care.

Ironically, the only problem is that to look decent for medical appointments may give the impression 'you *look* OK." - so must *be* OK'.

We do judge by appearances. We may not approve of that – but we do.

21. Set limits

You do not need to explain or justify setting limits on your time or energies. Your number one priority has to be to keep your own sanity. But try not to give out any message to invite sympathy – you might just feel angry if you don't get it!

If you are not able to cope, you have to pass the burden on when you can.

To limit her feeling of being overwhelmed, one woman tells her elderly mother that she has so much time a week to give her.

She will shop or cook or talk with her – at her mother's choosing; but it has to be either/or in that afternoon of three hours which she makes available. So if her mother wants errands or household work doing, these jobs are done in the three hours she has allocated.

This sounds very calculating – it is exactly that. And the mother knows where she is, thinks about the demands she is making – and the daughter keeps her sanity.

You can't always do this – you may be a person with a very low guilt threshold. But being a saint is not always wise or even kind if you then crack up and can do nothing.

If you can't say no immediately, tell people you will get back to them. Give yourself space. If and when you break down – will that person be there for you?

Another key habit to consider is not to be over-involved in trying to change other people – just take them as they are. You do need to be you.

Reduce the time you spend with people who do not share your values. On the other had, if you can ignore certain things you will have a bigger social system.

22. Develop your skills for making acquaintances and friends

Depression, by definition, makes you withdraw. The usual advice is that you need to go out and be with people.

At its best, seeing a friend is a relaxation and comfort. You can be yourself. However, *making* friends is work. It takes energy, attentiveness, confidence and gradual self-revelation. People usually make friends with those they see most often.

Young children and teenagers make friends quickly; it gets harder later when people are more circumspect, busy or self conscious.

It is older people who tend to be more cautious about making friends, and less tolerant of the diverse characteristics of others. Or they have enough already.

"Joining" takes confidence and energy which a depressed person does not have. Long standing members of a group may not understand what it is like to be new and, ironically, some social groups are often composed of those who are not good at making friends – which is why they join a ready made group!

The suggestion to "make new friends" can ignore the difficulties. It is very hard to keep contacting strangers.

But you don't have to overwhelmingly like the other person for them to be your "friend" – you need people, and they can be "friends" at a lot of different levels as long as they share some of your interests or values. If you only see people you really and truly like all the time you might be quite lonely.

A depressed person has lost confidence. They don't think that other people want their company; searching for reassurance, they may apologise too often or see slights where none were intended. Try to behave as if the other person is really wanting to see or hear from you! But watch how people interact before you barge in, and if you are a very withdrawn person, try to focus on finding out about the other person by attending to what they say.

You might need to be solitary for a while when you are very depressed – but avoid being isolated as a way of life. You need to be in touch with people to keep hold of reality. When you are depressed, you are also over-sensitised to perceived rejections.

To sustain a real friendship you just have to 'get something back' – or it is not friendship. You might be doing good turns for people, but is not friendship unless it is reciprocated. If you have grown up not getting much in the way of good responses to your efforts, you can almost be programmed not to expect them.

You are the one others depend on, but they are never of any support to you. Then you may descend into loneliness and despair.

You may end up with fewer friends, not more. But you can keep some people as acquaintances. And, when you feel a lot better, try to keep doing stuff so you can meet other people, and hopefully one or two along the way will reciprocate.

Sharing an interest is the best way – it may be work or a hobby, something which brings you to the same place.

Even then, be realistic. When you are there, others may be glad to see you. When you are not, they may not notice. Don't dwell on it.

23. Learn to have fun

Earlier we met the character called **'Little Pink Riding Hood'** - who is, of course, a paler and sadder version of Little Red Riding Hood and described by Eric Berne in *Games People Play* - waiting around until people she can help come along, such as the more fun-loving Little Red Riding Hood, whom she forlornly warns about the Big Bad Wolf……

The Little Pink Riding Hood is heading for serious depression. She is the 'helpful child', and is both a rescuer of others and also a victim. She thinks people only like her because of what she does to help them. She never has any fun herself. She does not get invited to fun things either.

She "rescues" people by nurturing, advising, supporting, but then becomes a "sad child" – and very angry when she finds that she is alone herself when people are either not grateful or not responsive – or even resentful.

The Pink Riding Hood character has been taught as a child to do her duty and not complain, to be helpful to people. But she is feels that she tries and gets nowhere, feels abandoned and neglected.

The antidote is that she needs to use her "adult brain" – her imagination – to do something for herself. She might have grown up thinking this is "selfish". She has to re-train her brain.

You need to start behaving - acting - *as if* you are OK. You are almost playing a role.

24. Create a personal story: re-invent yourself

This may sound odd. But many people do not tell the whole untarnished truth about themselves. Others tend to take you at your own presentation.

One of the most difficult factors with severe depression may be the history which has made you vulnerable. This is not just about your own depression, but your background such as abuse or major family problems.

For whatever reason, you can feel yourself to be a victim. And you might well have been a victim.

However, you may be misunderstood if you try to share this in any way. You may need to construct yourself, to present yourself as a 'together' person, in order to meet other more equally together people, rather than those who drain you.

This does not mean you cannot "be yourself" – but you choose which self you want to be. You don't have to tell people everything.

Otherwise, others may be talking about their "normal" mothers, fathers, children, grandchildren, – all the paraphernalia of saying " this is my tribe, this is where I belong", and you don't have the same currency. You can listen for a short time, be a small part of someone else's world.

If you have a nightmare relative, or several, you don't actually need to tell others all the details. However much we might dislike it, people make judgements and draw conclusions quickly. "Be yourself" is OK advice if you are a star, but not if your dad is the local drug dealer.

You may at some point have to be circumspect about how much you reveal. Don't dwell on health or how rubbish you are at something.

25. Use Imagination and Modelling

We can create ourselves with our imagination. So, for example, if you see someone you admire, you can think about what it is that you like about them and try to imagine what that person does in their spare time, how they organise themselves, how they talk to other people.

We send out signals, often automatically. We can invite respect or contempt and rejection by the way we show ourselves to others. When we feel a lot better, and to avoid the depression trap again, we can look at people who get respect. How do they do that? They may well have had a better start in life, more advantages – but you can take some lessons.

Once we feel better in using our imagination we can improve our surroundings or start some small new activities which don't make too many demands. Goals, no matter how small, get us through the 'slough of despond'. But it does not have to be a big goal.

Try to find humour, colour, music. And the main thing is to *build such stuff into your life*, as a habit. Habits and routines are not boring – they help you through the bad times.

26. Adopt a pet

If you are alone in any way, think seriously about adopting a pet – as long as you can manage the care of it easily. Animal company is less complex than the human kind and can be a huge reassurance. Wolves were tamed not just to help the hunter but as companion animals.

CONCLUSIONS

Grief, loss of any kind, a lack of support and social isolation will pre-dispose anyone towards depression. Only when a person has actually experienced severe depression can they understand the unique feeling of separateness it creates.

Once you are severely depressed, you cannot even imagine that you will get better. Depression seems to leave you stranded in a parallel universe. You are not in need of cheering up but of healing, starting with getting the chemical balance right. **Your brain needs to re-set itself.**

The first challenge is not to damage yourself or anyone else whilst you are in the depths of the depression. Managing depression means **recognising that you are vulnerable** to the condition. You know that now. You accept who you are whilst trying to change what you do.

Medication, solitude, quietness, the passage of time – all help. And, when you can concentrate enough, read books which give support and some consolation.

"Rest, cure and removal from irritating persons" (Emile Kraepelin) has been suggested – a detox from certain people! You will already know who they are. Just admit it, that is all. **Your expectations of friends have to be realistic,** and you may review just how much those around you really do you any good... Just as we can't usually expect a friend to set a broken leg, so they may not to be much help with a severe depression. They may even contribute to its onset.

Don't spend long with people you know have a negative effect on you – use a timer, another appointment, anything at all to restrict the time you are exposed to the stress. Plan in advance. Don't be taken over by other people's agenda: it is your responsibility to have your own.

One very recent event continued the writer's own learning about her coping capacities.

Having been managing reasonably well for some time, she had a friend to stay. When the friend left, after three days, the writer felt exhausted yet unable to sleep and, the following day, deeply disturbed and dispirited.

What had happened? Nothing dramatic. The had friend talked of her holidays, her children, her parents, her other friends, her life in general, but she had no interest in the writer's life except as a hook on which to hang further chat about her own. The writer had become exhausted both in the effort she had made to entertain the friend and in feeling that her own life was of no interest at all to the friend.

She had set aside her own "life" and later admitted to herself that she had become tired, bored and angry. But her friend cannot be anything other than she is.

We don't need to get 'get rid of' all these not-very-good friends, just detach ourselves a little more. At the same time, we need to explore further afield.

We have to cultivate indifference, an *apathaia*. Hate and disillusion bind you; but '**indifference' sets you free.** You need one person to care about, but not necessarily that one particular person forever.

Managing Severe Depression

The very first stages of depression, such as lying in bed in the mornings, 'rumination' or wrestling with strange remembered dreams, are attractive to start with. ***"What exactly are you doing now?"*** is a good question to ask yourself – out loud. It is the voice of your inner self, your ego.

We may be pre-disposed to some reactions. **Genetic factors make it more difficult for some persons to effectively cope with prolonged stress,** and make them more likely to explode in anger or slide into despondency (Levi, p.267) But we can become aware of our vulnerabilities and manage our lives as best we can.

Mind and body are linked – if you are depressed, you are more like to get ill, and vice versa. Once you are over the very worst, try to force yourself to become curious about the world outside your own.

You need to build what is called a "hinterland" – areas of interest. Assuming you are not working, at first you can only rest and get through the day. You may be able to go and buy a newspaper: then, maybe, to have a coffee somewhere.

Do that at the same time every day. Build a routine. And keep adding slowly to that routine. If you are working, you need diversions, even if you are tired, or your mind will get working on insolubles.

Daylight helps – it does not "cure" serious depression – but it does help the slow recovery. **Go out in the daylight.**

People seem to need love, work – however you define work - and a connection to something bigger than themselves. **You need to have your basic survival needs met** – somewhere to live and something to eat.

Other people behave in ways even they do not understand. But their behaviour can change yours; you may react to defend yourself, to attack, to complain. You are also echoing your emotions about your earlier life of rejection, loss or neglect   Do we know how others feel in our presence? They don't usually tell us. We may even be envied – which comes as a surprise to some people. You can dwell on things or use your brain to **move away from an unproductive puzzle of human behaviour. Shrug as best you can. That shrug is vital for survival.**

There is an intriguing sense in which, in each of us, **there is a separate "self" which can be drawn on** and which is slightly outside the depression. Styron calls it the sense of being accompanied by a second self, which does not share the dementia. (p.64)

It is useful if you begin to recognise patterns. The morning is the time when distortions are most likely and other symptoms of depression are often greater at the start of the day, and it gradually improves (e.g. see Whybrow, p.144). But find your own pattern.

The feeling of solitariness may be realistic. We may need something to come home to …but it doesn't have to be human. Any living creature - something which seems to need you and responds in a more consistent and predictable way than humans - can give a real boost to morale. **We also need a distraction and an occupation** of some kind – preferably outside the home.

Managing Severe Depression

You may now know that you cannot turn to certain people for help. You do not need to be upset again. Accept the reality.

It is sad but it is not a disaster. It is disappointing but it is not fatal. It is annoying but you can survive it.

You become more centred and grounded on your own life which you can build, or re-build, brick by brick.

Then look after it.

CONTACTS

SAMARITANS - offers a 24/7 listening service staffed by trained volunteers 08457 909090, or by e mail jo@samaritans.org and also by postal letters to Chris, PO Box 90, Stirling, FK8 28A.. Some areas run a drop in office in town centres

DEPRESSION ALLIANCE
information@depressionalliance.org offers free leaflets on relevant topics with pen friends and support groups.

MIND – campaigning group, covering a wide range of mental conditions and sometimes taking up Government sponsored initiatives, and approaches from researchers and the media   029 2039 5123 or e-mail contact@mind.org.uk

PRIORY CLINICS – private hospitals and clinics in various parts of the country staffed by psychiatrists and support staff covering mental health, addictions and learning difficulties. Will also do private assessment reports.   0845 477 4679 e mail info@priorygroup.com

SANE – runs a London based volunteer staffed helpline and campaign group. Started in 1986 by Marjorie Wallace with a Times endeavour to end the stigma of mental illness. Saneline, 6 p.m. – 11 p.m.   020 735 1002 info@sane.org.ik

REFERENCES

ARRANZ, Mattias, quoted in *The Times Register*, September 22, 2008

BERNE, Eric, *"Games People Play"* Pan Books, London 1987

BURTON, Robert, *The Anatomy of Melancholy* (1621) New York Review of Books, 2001

CARRUTHERS, Wallace, *FT Weekend* November 29/30, 2008

DE BEAUVOIR, Simone, *'All Said and Done'*, Penguin Modern Classics, 1972, p. 69

DURKHEIM, Emile, *"On Suicide"* (1897) Penguin Classics, 2006

GARVEY, Guy, *Elbow*. The South Bank Show, 15 November, 2009

GLADWELL, Malcolm, *"Outliers: the Story of Success"* Allen Lane, 2008

GRIFFFIN, Joe, Mindfields College, *How to communicate more effectively* www.mindfields.org.uk (training manuscript, undated)

HAIDT, Jonathan, *The Happiness Hypothesis,* Heinemann, 2006

HAMBURG, David A, Hamburg, Beatrice and Barchus, Jack D, Raven Press New York 1975 in *Emotions Their Parameters and Measurement* (Lennart Levi, ed)

INGRAM, Dr Mike, We need a change of heart on statins (?) *"I don't have one of those affluent happy lifestyles I see all about me. Can I please have a happy pill?"* (Daily Telegraph, 4 Sept, 2008, p. 20)

KRISHNAMURTI, J, *Freedom from the Known*, Victor Golanz, 1969, p. 12

LAKE, Tony, *Loneliness*, Sheldon Press, 1980

LEADER, Darian, *The New Black, Mourning, Melancholia and Depression*, Hamish Hamilton, 2008

MILLER, Jean Baker, *Towards a New Psychology of Women*, 1976, p. 67

PLANT, Jane and STEPHENSON, Janet *Beating Stress, Anxiety and Depression,* Piatkus, 2008 (lengthy but readable and good for milder depression)

NEWBY, Eric, *Love and War in the Apennines* Hodder and Stoughton, 1971, p. 116

STYRON, William, *Darkness Visible*, Picador, 1990

KOLODIEJCHUK, Brian, (ed), Mother Teresa of Calcutta, *Come be my light*, Rider, 2008

WEST, Rebecca, *Black Lamb and Grey Falcon*, MacMillan, 1942

WHYBROW, Peter, A Mood Apart, *A Thinker's Guide to Emotion and Its Disorders*, Picador, 1997 (lots of interesting ideas)

WOLPERT, Lewis *Malignant Sadness. The Anatomy of Depression,* Faber and Faber, 1999

www.ingramcontent.com/pod-product-compliance
Ingram Content Group UK Ltd.
Pitfield, Milton Keynes, MK11 3LW, UK
UKHW041412180426
11947UKWH00007B/81